Conecting the Dots

The Life of an Academic Lawyer

HARRY W. ARTHURS

McGill-Queen's University Press
Montreal & Kingston • London • Chicago
and
The Osgoode Society for Canadian Legal History
Toronto

© McGill-Queen's University Press 2019

ISBN 978-0-7735-5709-3 (cloth)
ISBN 978-0-7735-5757-4 (ePDF)
ISBN 978-0-7735-5758-1 (ePUB)

Legal deposit second quarter 2019
Bibliothèque nationale du Québec

Printed in Canada on acid-free paper that is 100% ancient forest free
(100% post-consumer recycled), processed chlorine free

We acknowledge the support of the Canada Council for the Arts.
Nous remercions le Conseil des arts du Canada de son soutien.

Library and Archives Canada Cataloguing in Publication

Title: Conecting the dots : the life of an academic lawyer / Harry W. Arthurs.
Names: Arthurs, H. W. (Harry William), 1935– author.
Description: Includes bibliographical references and index.
Identifiers: Canadiana (print) 20190048212 | Canadiana (ebook) 2019004828X
  | ISBN 9780773557093 (hardcover) | ISBN 9780773557574 (ePDF) | ISBN
  9780773557581 (ePUB)
Subjects: LCSH: Arthurs, H. W. (Harry William), 1935– | LCSH: Law teachers—
  Canada—Biography. | LCSH: College teachers—Canada—Biography. | LCSH:
  Lawyers—Canada—Biography. | LCGFT: Autobiographies.
Classification: LCC KE416.A78 A3 2019 | LCC KF345.Z9 A78 2019 kfmod | DDC
  340.092—dc23

This book was typeset in 10.5/13 Sabon.

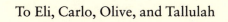

To Eli, Carlo, Olive, and Tallulah

Contents

Foreword

Harry Arthurs has been a centrally important figure in Canadian legal education for more than fifty years. He came to national prominence as a scholar and educator in the 1960s and 1970s with his seminal writing on labour law. In the 1970s, he was dean of Osgoode Hall Law School, and in 1983 he was principally responsible for *Law and Learning*, the most important report on legal education in the past half century. From 1985 to 1992 he was president of York University. He has also served on many government commissions investigating labour law, and as the president of the Canadian Civil Liberties Association. In addition, he has written extensively on legal history, the legal profession, and legal education, with a special emphasis on the effect of globalization on the latter two areas. This account of Arthurs's intellectual trajectory, more of a "life and times" than an autobiography, is the memoir of a person who has lived his professional life to the full and rendered his country much meritorious service. It covers all aspects of his career, a compendium of trials, tribulations, and triumphs, with frankness, perspicacity, and humour. Readers will learn about the "blacks arts" of academic administration as well as why Arthurs can call himself a "useful idiot"!

The purpose of the Osgoode Society for Canadian Legal History is to encourage research and writing in the history of Canadian law. The Society, which was incorporated in 1979 and is registered as a charity, was founded at the initiative of the Honourable R. Roy McMurtry and officials of the Law Society of Upper Canada. The society seeks to stimulate the study of legal history in Canada by supporting researchers, collecting oral histories, and publishing volumes that contribute to legal-historical scholarship. This year's books bring the total published since 1981 to 109, in all fields of legal history – the courts, the judiciary, and the legal profession, as well as on the history of crime and punishment, women and law, law and economy, the legal treatment of ethnic minorities, and famous cases and significant trials.

Current directors of the Osgoode Society for Canadian Legal History are Heidi Bohaker, Bevin Brooksbank, Shantona Chaudhury, David Chernos, Linda Silver Dranoff, Michael Fenrick, Timothy Hill, Ian Hull, Trisha Jackson, Mahmud Jamal, Virginia MacLean, Waleed Malick, Rachel McMillan, Roy McMurtry, Malcolm Mercer, Caroline Mulroney, Dana Peebles, Paul Reinhardt, William Ross, Paul Schabas, Robert Sharpe, Jon Silver, Alex Smith, Lorne Sossin, Mary Stokes, and Michael Tulloch.

Robert J. Sharpe
President

Jim Phillips
Editor-in-Chief

CONNECTING THE DOTS

To Write or Not to Write?

Autobiography is an odd art form. If it's too personal and intimate, it becomes an exercise in auto-eroticism; if it's not personal enough, if it's the history of a one-dimensional public or professional life, it lacks authenticity. Worse yet, autobiography depends on sources that can't be depended upon – on paper records that are often fragmentary or sometimes missing altogether, or on the author's memory that inevitably plays tricks and, with advancing years, becomes friskier and friskier. And worst of all, in my case at least, autobiography may be surplus to requirements. I have published a couple of mini-memoirs,[1] been memorialized by colleagues in a review article, a symposium, and a *festschrift*,[2] and age gracefully in several archives.[3] Does posterity really need more of me?

Nonetheless, autobiography is an art form with certain attractions. If begun as a diary early in one's life (which this one was not), it instils in the author habits of self-reflection; if undertaken in retirement as a way of filling hours in a formerly crowded schedule (which this one was), it affords an opportunity for honest reminiscence about, or consoling revision of, what was and what might have been. And finally, autobiography is not just for the autobiographer: it provides fodder for discussion by the other *dramatis personae* as well as footnotes for subsequent serious historians. These are persuasive arguments, and I've almost convinced myself to begin.

Almost: but not quite. If I do decide to write something, it is not going to be an autobiography in the strict sense of the word – "an account of a person's life written by that person." Rather than writing about my life I want to write about my life's work, about the events, ideas, and people that shaped it, about whether I've made a difference.

Reader: do we have an understanding? I'm not going to take you on the usual autobiographer's ramble through the thickets of childhood and adolescence, the lush forest of adult relationships, or the broad sunlit uplands (or bleak tundra) of dotage and decline. I'm not going to say much about love, friendship, or obsession, about pride, regret, or resentment. This work-focused approach exposes me to the risk of sounding unidimensional and inauthentic, as I've acknowledged. But I promise to link events in my career to my private life whenever the two are intertwined, and to be as frank about my public and professional adventures as libel laws and good taste permit.

Agreed? A deal? Good! I'll begin at the beginning. No, on second thought, I'll begin *before* the beginning.

Before the Beginning, and My Life So Far

BEFORE THE BEGINNING

My maternal grandparents were remarkable people. Harry Dworkin emigrated to Toronto circa 1905 from the Ukraine, where his family was involved in the tobacco business. He was nineteen or so when he joined two of his siblings who had come earlier. Very soon, he and his brother Edward opened a tobacco, stationery, and sundries shop in St John's Ward, where Jewish immigrants from Eastern Europe settled at the beginning of the twentieth century. A second business followed – Dworkin's Jewish Advertising Bureau – and then, in 1917, a third, E & H Dworkin travel agency.

Shortly after the end of World War I, Harry began a series of trips to Eastern Europe to organize trainloads of immigrants – mostly women and children being reunited with a male relative who had gone ahead to establish himself in Canada in the expectation (delayed by the war) that he would soon send for the rest of his family. This business flourished to the point where Harry had an agent and a secretary in Warsaw making local arrangements including purchasing tickets, contacting passengers, making arrangements for them to assemble on a specified departure date, and other logistical matters. Harry himself visited some of the major cities in Poland to contact prospective clients; according to his letters, on one occasion he was the guest of honour at a civic reception and a poem dedicated to him appeared in a local newspaper.

One major source of profit for the travel agency was currency exchange. The Canadian family member would pay for the passengers' fares in strong currency, while the actual ticket was purchased locally in Polish, Russian, or another currency weakened by rampant inflation and international tensions. (A sign in the window at 525 Dundas Street West, where they had relocated their businesses, proclaimed E & H Dworkin to be "bankers" as well as travel agents.) However, these arrangements entailed the risk that the foreign currency would become worthless. Moreover, the difficulty of transferring funds in the postwar and pre-technology era led to the accumulation of currency overseas, which became a target for fraud and extortion. Harry fell victim to just such behaviour. His Warsaw agent received money Harry had wired from Canada but pocketed the funds rather than purchasing tickets with them. Upon receiving complaints from passengers who hadn't received their tickets, Harry went to Warsaw to straighten things out. He was promptly detained and held under house arrest. When he appealed to Edward to send funds so that he could resolve the situation, Edward, for some reason, refused. This led Harry to write that "we will always be brothers, but from this moment onward we are no longer business partners." In the end, my grandmother Dora had to go to Poland to rescue him, taking with her sufficient money to either pay a fine, bribe the police, or compensate the victims – which I'm not sure.

As I'll recount below, Harry's "banking" activities carried another risk as well. The RCMP suspected him of providing funds to the Polish Bolsheviks.[1] But despite these difficulties, Dworkin's travel agency flourished – not least because of Harry's deep concern for his clients. Letters from Harry to Dora provide an account of his first trip to Poland in September 1920. The timing of the trip was clearly inopportune, as the newly independent Polish state was at war with Soviet Russia (the fighting lasted until October of that year) and the adjacent Baltic countries were also in turmoil. Nonetheless, Harry collected some 200 immigrants and put them on board a chartered train for Antwerp, from where the passengers were to set sail to Canada. Alas, the train was sequestered as a result of a military development. Harry recounts that he contacted a French general attached to the Allied Control Commission who arranged for the train to be released, but when it reached the German border, it was denied passage through that country. Undaunted, Harry appealed to the British consul in Hamburg, who despatched a special train to take the travellers to their destination. By the time the train finally reached Antwerp, however, the ship on which they had booked passage had already sailed. "Everyone cried," writes Harry, "but I took them to the movies and bought them ice cream and they were happy." He also arranged for them to take the next available ship, and accompanied them overseas to Halifax and then by train to Toronto.

Harry, then, was a daring and successful businessman. A photo of him *en route* to Europe on another occasion shows him as a well-dressed and rather portly member of a party of Cunard Line booking agents; in one of his letters, he seems bemused by the company he is keeping and laments the fact that he has not brought his dinner jacket with him. On this trip, he made a detour to Paris, by which he was intrigued. His business was thriving, and by 1922, Harry and Dora had purchased a lot in Regal Heights, a prestigious development in what was then Toronto's outer suburbs near St Clair and Dufferin. They built a sizeable duplex (where I lived until I was seventeen), one floor of which was occupied until their death by my grandmother's parents. When the family first moved there, there was an orchard on the property with a stream running through it, and my mother's friends would come to visit for the weekend. By the time of Harry's death, in 1928, my grandparents had also acquired a number of investment properties, including substantial residences on High Park Boulevard and Russell Hill Road, three run-down houses on Miller Street in the Junction, and at least one in Long Branch, in what is now Etobicoke, Toronto's western borough.

Harry was no ordinary businessman. He provided goods to poor people "on the cuff" or for free, and even allowed those who were homeless to sleep in the Dworkin brothers' shop. The shop soon became a hub of community activity and the venue for vigorous debates amongst members of its numerous nationalist, radical, progressive, and anarchist sects.[2] Nor was Harry a mere bystander in these discussions. He and my grandmother were founding members of the Toronto chapter of the Workmen's Circle, a Jewish socialist group, and were active in various Jewish political and humanitarian causes, such as relief for Jewish refugees.

My grandparents were devoutly secular; indeed, they were militantly anti-religious and provoked observant Jews by organizing dances on the street in front of a synagogue during High Holiday services. Nonetheless, their commitment to the Jewish community was profound. Harry served on the provisional board of the Federation of Jewish Philanthropies of Toronto, as a volunteer collector for the Conference for Jewish War Sufferers, and as a delegate to the founding convention of the Canadian Jewish Congress at the Monument National in Montreal in 1919.[3] Harry's most passionate involvement with the Jewish community was with its labour movement, whose members largely worked in the garment factories located up and down Spadina Avenue, just steps away from the Dworkin travel agency. My mother recalled being taken to the Don Jail every Friday evening, where she watched her father bail out imprisoned strikers so that they could spend the Sabbath with their families. Along with a colleague, Sam Easser, he raised funds in 1924 to purchase two houses on Spadina Avenue which were converted into the Labour Lyceum, a meeting hall for the garment trades unions and other labour and socialist groups. Harry subsequently became chairman of the board of trustees that administered the Lyceum.[4]

Harry was also actively involved in civic politics. In 1915 – aged about thirty, just ten years after arriving in Canada – he ran unsuccessfully as a Labour candidate for city council. Subsequently he became a supporter of James Simpson, a trade unionist and future mayor of Toronto, who was prominent in several social democratic / labour parties. Though these somewhat ephemeral parties were clearly anti-communist, they were seen in some quarters as a threat to the established order. Consequently, in 1920, the RCMP placed Harry under surveillance as a subversive. Reports of the "red squad" – the Criminal Investigation Bureau (CIB) – claimed that Harry had travelled to Poland with a person described as a "dangerous agitator," that he himself was "pro-Bolshevist" and opposed to the right-wing Polish government then at war with the Soviet Union, and that he addressed "suspicious meetings" following his return from Poland. Subsequent RCMP reports suggest that he was arrested in Poland for pro-Bolshevik activity (he was indeed arrested, but apparently because of the theft of passengers' funds as recounted above) and that he was "a frequent speaker in Polish Communist circles."[5]

Were these suspicions justified? The RCMP reports acknowledge that Harry denied publicly, at a meeting in Welland, that he was a Bolshevik. Given his close association with the social democratic Labour party and with Jimmy Simpson, its aggressively anti-communist leader, this denial was almost certainly truthful. On the other hand, while the RCMP was clearly over-reacting to a perceived "red menace" in the wake of the Russian revolution and the Winnipeg general strike, political alignments on the left were notoriously ephemeral, alliances formed and dissolved relatively frequently, and at any given time who was opposed to whom and why may have been unclear.

On Friday, 13 January 1928, Harry parked his car on the south side of Queen Street, near John Street. He was due to go to a meeting of the Labour Lyceum board but had an errand to run first. Crossing Queen Street he was run over by a drunk driver, and died of his injuries while being admitted to hospital shortly afterwards. His funeral took place at the Lyceum rather than in a synagogue. According to newspaper reports some 18,000 people attended, including significant segments of the labour movement and much of the Jewish community. Someone who was present that day told me that Irish policemen on horseback beat the crowd back with batons, to allow passage of the cortège. "Out of the way, ye heathen!" they shouted. "Have ye no respect for the dead?"

"The dead" in question – Harry – was, to the contrary, very much respected not only by the thousands who came to bid him farewell but especially by his widow, my grandmother Dora Goldstick.[6] She was born circa 1890 in the small Baltic port of Windau in the then-Russian province of Courland/Kurland (now Ventspils in Latvia). Her parents were observant Jews who lived just outside of town and eked out a modest living dealing in fish and timber. Following a wave of pogroms in Russia, the family emigrated first to Sweden and then to Toronto, arriving in 1904.

The Goldstick siblings were a remarkable lot. One brother – Isadore – secured a PhD in modern languages, taught briefly at Upper Canada College, replacing a teacher who had gone off to war, and then moved to London, Ontario, where he became the long-serving head of modern languages at Central High School, and latterly taught at Western University. Isadore was also a translator and critic of Yiddish literature, and published a book on the Hebrew poet Yehoash, who was distantly related to Harry Dworkin. A second brother – David – first secured an engineering degree and then became a lawyer, one of the few to represent unions in the 1930s; he too ran unsuccessfully for city council. Dora's two remaining brothers – Maurice and Edward – trained as watchmakers and at various times worked in a watch factory in Waltham, Massachusetts, as itinerant peddlers and shopkeepers in rural Ontario, and as proprietors of a lumber and wrecking business in Toronto. Maurice was also the editor (and Dora the publisher) of *Kanada Neues/Canadian News* – a free Yiddish-English newspaper.

Dora's sisters were hardly less remarkable. Jean graduated from the University of Toronto, a rare achievement for an immigrant Jewish girl prior to 1920. Another sister, Betty, also a university graduate, became a schoolteacher and, like Harry Dworkin, was elected a delegate to the founding convention of the Canadian Jewish Congress. Of Dora's three remaining sisters, one died young; a second was widowed at an early age; and a third lived a humble life in Toronto's Junction neighbourhood.

Dora briefly attended school in Toronto and then went to work sewing buttonholes in a garment factory. However, she was soon identified as "promising," and sent to train as a nurse at Mount Sinai Hospital in Cleveland. Although a doctor in Cleveland suggested that she might go on to study medicine there, she returned to Toronto in 1909. This might seem like an odd decision on the part of an ambitious and able young woman, but a pile of love letters addressed to her in Cleveland by "Adolph," a suitor in Toronto, may provide the explanation. Back in Toronto, in fairly quick succession, she set up practice under the auspices of the Jewish Free Dispensary as the city's first Jewish registered nurse and midwife, ditched Adolph, and met and married Harry.

I do not know how my grandparents met, although their meeting seems almost inevitable, given that they were both rising stars in the progressive wing of Toronto's small Jewish community. In any event, they married in the summer of 1911 and had their only child, my mother Honey, in 1912. It must have been a marvellous marriage. By all accounts, Harry was handsome, lively, kind-hearted, and well-liked. My grandmother used to recall that he made it his business at parties to dance with "wallflowers" – unpopular young women with whom no one else would dance. And his generosity of spirit was a matter of public record: his obituary in the *Toronto Telegram* was headlined, "Won hearts by kindness."

Dora gave up nursing when she married Harry. Soon, however, she became involved in the Dworkin business ventures, which she managed during Harry's trips to Europe and, of course, after his death in 1928. The Dworkin Travel Agency was especially active during the 1930s, when Canadian Jewish families sought to rescue relatives from what some sensed was the looming disaster of Nazism. I know of one client who sought to book passage for a member of his large family in Europe; Dora urged him to bring everyone else as well and, when he said he couldn't afford to do so, she offered to give him the tickets on the understanding that he would pay for them when he was able. The entire family arrived in August 1939, just before the outbreak of World War II. The grateful client presented her with a silver brush, comb, and mirror, which always sat on her dressing room table. The family in question was named Daniels; they later became prominent in Toronto as developers, builders, and philanthropists.[7]

To its shame, the Canadian government was very reluctant to accept Jewish immigrants and, later, Jewish refugees.[8] Much of Dora's energy was therefore directed at persuading the immigration authorities to make exceptions to this policy. She met with politicians and civil servants; she lobbied influential people in the general community; and she cultivated the friendship and cooperation of local immigration staff. Her business flourished. After Israel was founded in 1948, she became El Al's principal Canadian agent; in the 1950s, she served as president of the Canadian Ticket Agents Association. The travel agency survived until her retirement in 1967 – the fiftieth anniversary of its foundation – although she became increasingly out of touch with a changing industry and more and more dependent on her small staff.

However, Dora's business activities were overshadowed by her work as a community activist. During the 1920s, she was a prime mover in a women's charitable group that provided support for orphans and the aged and, from 1923, for the campaign to establish the Mount Sinai Hospital. She was the hospital's treasurer through the 1920s and 1930s and also served as president of its ladies auxiliary.[9] And her activism did not stop there. Dora held executive positions in several organizations concerned with the plight of Jews in inter- and postwar Europe; she was an active board member of the Labour Lyceum, the Federation of Jewish Philanthropies, and the Jewish Labour Committee; and for good measure, she served as honorary treasurer of the local Bagel Makers Union. She was also the Toronto distributor of several New York Jewish newspapers and, as mentioned, the publisher of the *Kanada Neues* which, in turn, sponsored concerts to benefit various charities as well as the *Jewish Hour* radio program advertising Dworkin Travel. Finally, Dora served as an unofficial emissary to the larger polity. Thus, in the late 1930s, she held a reception at our home for Lord Marley, a visiting Labour peer and advocate of Jewish causes; she was friends with Herbert Mowat, a prominent Anglican layman and supporter of Zionism; and she worked closely for decades with Liberal senator Arthur Roebuck, a former Ontario attorney-general famous for refusing to order the police to break the General Motors strike in Oshawa in 1937.

Like Harry, then, Dora was a prominent citizen of the Jewish community and very active in its many organizations. And, like Harry, she held firm to her secular principles. She often recounted how she and her non-observant siblings would celebrate Passover with their beloved, observant – but aged, sight-impaired and hard-of-hearing – parents. While the younger generation honoured their parents by singing traditional melodies learned in childhood, they affirmed their atheism by chanting names from the Toronto phone book instead of the prescribed religious text.

This brief account of the lives of my remarkable grandparents, Harry and Dora,[10] raises a question that lies at the heart of any autobiography: what influences shaped the life of its principal subject (in this case me)? Clearly my grandparents – or the family legends that celebrated them – shaped my life to a considerable extent. My political beliefs and social values, like theirs, are not radical but progressive (though I confess to supporting individual candidates and working with governments from across the political spectrum); I share their aversion to religious observance (though I have never been as militantly irreverent as they were); it is no coincidence that, like them, I worked with the garment trades unions (though as a neutral rather than a partisan; see chapter 3); and I was quite involved in Jewish community affairs as a student and during my early career (though I abandoned my active participation in the late 1960s over an issue of principle, as I describe in chapter 4). It turns out that Harry and Dora even bequeathed me their entrepreneurial gene (which became manifest when, as university president, I established York University Development Corporation and became actively involved in its activities; see chapter 7).

There's no doubt, then, that my grandparents significantly shaped my character, my world view, and my values. What is less clear is how they accomplished this, given that my actual contact with them was limited. True, I am named after Harry, my grandmother spoke of him frequently, and his portrait hung over the mantel in our living room. But he died seven years before I was born. True as well, my parents, my sister, and I lived with Dora until I went off to graduate school in 1958. But she was away at business and community events six days a week, and on the seventh she would retreat to

her bedroom. There she took her well-earned rest and found refuge
from the turmoil of a household in whose affairs her influence was
waning. There too she could think about old times without being
reminded that, like most children, my sister and I had only limited
tolerance for her lugubrious rehearsal of the very family lore that
I have just recounted. I have to confess that Harry and Dora have
come alive for me – have become more interesting and impressive to
me – now that I can relate to them as historical figures rather than
as ephemeral presences and occasional irritants in the complicated,
sometimes tense, politics of our family.

MY LIFE SO FAR (IN 3,000 WORDS)

As I explained in my introduction, family politics will not loom
large in this autobiography; in fact, they will not loom at all. Inevitably, however, as I recount the story of my career, I must mention
them briefly.

I was born in 1935. My parents separated before I was two; my
mother remarried when I was five; and these events, combined with
her father's untimely death, cast a shadow over her life, and consequently to an extent over mine. Nonetheless, Honey – my mother
– never held grudges, was always supportive of me and my sister
Cindy, and loved her grandchildren extravagantly. Her worst fault
was that she never treated herself with the same generosity she
extended to others. My adoptive father Leon was a man of enor-
mous intelligence, fierce determination, and domineering tendencies
– a personality that did not always make for harmonious relations.
Forced to leave school at fourteen, he first became an electrician,
then in quick succession a salesman and inventor of medical devices
and, during the war, a radio technician who worked as a civilian
contractor for the army. Finally in 1946, in his mid-thirties, after
an intensive course of self-study, he passed the Canadian Patent
Office exams and began practice as a patent agent. He pursued this
career with great distinction, worked closely with leading lawyers
in Toronto and Ottawa, London, and Washington, and ensured that
even before I left high school, dinnertime conversation and summer
jobs had set me on the path to a career in law.

Indeed, what other profession could I possibly consider? From the
time I could form sentences (so I am told), I made speeches; in high
school in lawyer-like fashion I wrote essays, debated, and immersed

myself in student politics; and science – hence medicine and engineering – held little interest for me, even if I could have broken through the real and rumoured barriers that made it difficult for Jewish students to join those professions. In order to enter law school, I had first to earn an undergraduate degree. I foolishly enrolled in the general arts course at the University of Toronto, which would get me to law school in three years instead of the four required for a specialized honours degree. I wish now that I had spent the extra year (and perhaps done graduate work as well), but at least I arrived at law school with a modest smattering of history, political science, and economics, an introduction to anthropology and psychology, and whatever extracurricular inspiration I could glean from the meagre social, cultural, and political offerings of campus life in those rather dreary years of the 1950s.

Law school, then, was preordained. However, study at the University of Toronto's Faculty of Law was not. Until 1949, graduation from Osgoode Hall Law School – run by the profession's governing body, the Law Society of Upper Canada[11] – was the only point of entry to the Ontario bar. However, in that year, Toronto's undergraduate law department was reconstituted as a full-fledged faculty of law whose graduates would receive an education comparable to and arguably better than that offered at Osgoode. Unfortunately, until the late 1950s, the Law Society continued to deny Toronto graduates full credit for their law degrees. As a result, they had to retake certain courses and spend an extra year becoming qualified for practice. This discouraged many aspiring lawyers from enrolling in Toronto's Faculty of Law. On the other hand, those of us who did so were fiercely committed to the notion that our legal education was vastly superior to what was on offer at the Law Society's "trade school."

And in fact it was. The University of Toronto's nine professors constituted the largest full-time legal-academic complement in the country; their preferred pedagogy – the now-discredited Socratic or "case" method of instruction – was then considered cutting edge; they sought to reform the law through constructive and well-reasoned criticism of legislation and judicial decisions; they contributed to the education of the profession by editing law reports and scholarly journals and by writing articles and case-notes (though seldom treatises or monographs); and not least, they tried to liberate their students intellectually from the uninspiring mixture of conceptualism and "war stories" that prevailed at the rival institution, by preaching (though seldom practising) legal realism. In short, Toronto's Faculty of Law in the 1950s could properly be described as Canada's most progressive law school, even though it might not be regarded as such by today's standards.

Its students could fairly be described as a self-selected elite as well. The tiny classes of the 1950s included at least two future members of the Supreme Court of Canada and numerous judges of other courts, many leading politicians and business executives, a number of distinguished academics and civil servants, as well as practitioners in almost every branch of the legal profession. My own four-person study group, which met every Sunday for three years, included two future law deans (myself and Martin Friedland), a senator (Jerry Grafstein), and a president of the Ontario Bar Association (Harvey Bliss). But to repeat, students at the University of Toronto Law school were *self*-selected: no minimum GPA to ensure we were high achievers; no LSAT to test our analytical abilities; and consequently, a high attrition rate that reduced my own entering cohort of students from almost fifty to just over thirty by the end of first year.

I was almost a contributor to that dismal statistic. I couldn't see the point of common law reasoning. I didn't realize that "radical" perspectives like legal realism were designed to enable one to talk the talk in law school; when one walked the walk, it was technical legal analysis that counted. On the practice exams we wrote at Christmas in first year, I managed to score 23 per cent in Dean Wright's Torts course and earned his exasperated notation of "horse-feathers" on my exam script. Somehow, with the aid of my study group, I managed to pull myself together and performed respectably on the finals. At the end of second year, I made a decision that probably changed my life, or at least provided a glimpse into how it would unfold. Martin Friedland invited me to join him as co-editor of the law review; I accepted, and abandoned my campaign to be class president. While politics (in the broadest sense) continued to engage me both intellectually and as a practitioner, my stint as an editor showed me that I could and should remain anchored in scholarly work and perspectives.

In any event, by the end of third year I could give a passable imitation of a competent student and graduated second or third in my class. My class standing, however, mattered much less to me than the fact that I was awarded the Labour Law prize. As noted, my maternal grandparents, though successful in business, had been strong supporters of unions; my grandmother's brother was one of the few Toronto lawyers who would represent unions in the 1930s; and my favourite professor was Bora Laskin – one of Canada's pioneering labour law academics, a future chief justice of Canada, and my mentor and role model.[12] I left law school with a passion for labour law, but no clear idea of how to pursue it. Luckily for me, someone suggested that I go to graduate school. This would not only enhance my knowledge of the field; it would postpone the moment when I would need to decide on a career. Like so many Canadian legal academics before me (and since), I enrolled in the master of laws program at Harvard Law School, where I attended labour law courses offered by Archibald Cox (later JFK's solicitor general and Watergate special prosecutor) and Derek Bok (later dean of the law school and president of Harvard University). I learned a great deal from both of them, and from encounters with Lon Fuller, a leading legal theorist, and Albert Sacks, an administrative lawyer and co-founder of the "legal process" school, of whom more in subsequent chapters. But at the end of my year at Harvard, I was no closer to choosing a career path than I had been at the beginning.

I decided to serve my year under articles, a necessary step towards admission to the bar, and was offered several attractive opportunities. Happily, I decided to article for Sydney Robins, himself a Harvard LLM graduate, a part-time lecturer at Osgoode Hall Law School, an excellent advocate, and one of a relatively small cadre of labour specialists who represented union-side clients. Robins gave me a great deal of responsibility, opened my eyes to many practical and psychological aspects of legal practice, and introduced me to what I can only describe as "labour law without tears" – a sympathetic perspective on unions and their legal travails that nonetheless included an honest assessment of their shortcomings. As I completed my training and approached my call to the bar, he asked me to join his firm. I was strongly tempted to do so but almost at the same moment, I learned that Osgoode was looking for someone to teach labour law. I applied and got the job – my first real job, and the one I have held all through my career and now still hold (notionally) as a professor emeritus.

Still, joining the Osgoode faculty was not an obvious career choice. On the one hand, the possibility of an academic career had never crossed my mind – understandably, since in 1961 there were well under one hundred full-time law professors in all of Canada.

On the other, my legal education at the University of Toronto left me convinced of Osgoode's many shortcomings, epitomized as it happens by the hard-nosed anti-intellectual anti-union part-time lecturer whose departure left the vacancy my appointment would fill. However, Osgoode was beginning to change. The Law Society had decided in 1957 to give full faith and credit to University of Toronto degrees (and those of several new Ontario law schools). Osgoode itself was becoming a more conventional law school, lacking only a university affiliation. And the ranks of legal academe were beginning to be filled by a new generation of scholars who looked and thought very much as I did.

As things turned out, the decade of change at Osgoode following my appointment coincided with transformational developments in law and legal education more generally, and with that era of social, political, and cultural turmoil known as "the sixties." I soon found my inner radical. I pointedly declined to give formal lectures to my labour law class and began my first-ever class with a documentary film about a strike; incensed by the unfair denial of tenure to a deserving colleague, I organized a local unit of the Canadian Association of University Teachers; I published a muted criticism of a Court of Appeal judgment ("an affirmation of totalitarian philosophy")[13] that led to the author's (and my dean's) demand that I apologize; and I espoused an unconventional perspective on constitutional law that led a senior colleague to persuade the dean that I should never be allowed to teach the subject. Still, my career flourished. My classes went well. I published extensively (at least by the standards of the day). I soon earned tenure and was promoted. Then, in the spring of 1965, I received job offers from two leading Canadian law schools – McGill and Toronto.

Though tempted by these offers, I was even more attracted by the opportunity that had suddenly materialized at Osgoode. In March 1965, the Law Society announced that as of 1968, its law school would become affiliated with the recently established York University and would relocate to its suburban campus. This seemed to me to be a heaven-sent opportunity to put into practice some of the progressive ideas about law, legal education, and legal scholarship that had begun to percolate at Osgoode. When the incumbent dean and several senior faculty members vehemently denounced the move to York, I became the self-styled coordinator of the affiliation project and, working with other young faculty members, became deeply involved in bringing it to a successful conclusion.[14] This led in January 1968 to my appointment by our new dean, Gerald Le Dain, as his associate dean, and then in 1972 to my selection as his successor. After ending my own deanship in 1977, I spent seven happy years immersed in highly productive academic work. True, I made several excursions into public and professional affairs: I became a member of the Economic Council of Canada, a bencher of the Law Society of Upper Canada, and chair of the Consultative Group on Research and Education in Law, which conducted the first-ever comprehensive Canadian study of those subjects.[15] For much of that time, however, I was hard at work on my most significant book, "*Without the Law*," a study of the emergence of the administrative state in nineteenth-century England.[16]

Then, quite unexpectedly, I was appointed president of York University – so unexpectedly, in fact, that the job was offered to me in late June 1984, just ten days before my scheduled departure for a year's research leave in England. Spirited negotiations ensued; I agreed to take just half my leave and to assume York's presidency in January 1985; and my family agreed to manage without me for six months, from that January until the following June when our sons would complete their school year in London.

Being president was in many ways the greatest challenge of my career – not (I like to think) because I was in a position of power or found that I had a talent for its exercise but because, for me, university administration at the senior level turned out to be a continuation of scholarship by other means. I enrolled (metaphorically speaking) in the School of Black Arts, majoring in "leadership," fundraising, lobbying, and networking. I took crash courses in finance, architecture, information technology, corporate governance, and time management – subjects any York president would need to master. I upgraded my previous academic training as a labour and administrative lawyer by engaging in practical exercises in dispute resolution and systems-building. But best of all, my interactions with colleagues from across the university enabled me to absorb smatterings of biology, literary theory, economics, astrophysics, urbanism, and ancient history. Somehow these smatterings all came together, and I left my presidency with much broader intellectual perspectives than I entered it.

Needless to say, I also left it exhausted. However, after a year's research leave (at my old academic home, the University of Toronto law faculty), I soon found my scholarly stride again. Indeed, I not only found it but strode faster and farther than I ever had before. The years following my presidency have been the most productive of my academic career – the result, I do not doubt, of having been away from law and immersed in other domains of learning for an extended period. I never have returned to a major administrative post despite receiving a few tentative approaches – to take up another presidency, to become dean of a rising American law school, to assume some role in government, to join a major law firm. Instead, as I describe in chapter 9, I have taken on a series of one-off commissions and committee assignments in both the university sector and in the broader public sphere. The three most important of these were as a sole commissioner reviewing federal labour standards legislation (2004–2006), Ontario's workplace pension system (2006–2008), and the funding of its workers' compensation scheme (2010–2012). This was challenging work, and I feel that my reports contributed to the development of sound public policies in these three fields (a sentiment not necessarily shared by the governments to whom I reported). However, the major focus of my post-presidential years has been scholarship.

I have already suggested that my intellectual horizons expanded considerably during my presidency. During those same years, events in the academy and in the wider world were ringing the changes in legal scholarship. After law's extended encounters with post-modernism, with critical theories of class, gender, and race, with varieties of liberal theory and economic analysis, and with interdisciplinarity in general, most legal academics would no longer accept Justice Holmes's assertion (radical for its time) that law is simply "prophecies of what the courts will do in fact."[17] And after law's reshaping by the forces of neo-liberalism and globalization, many legal academics began to revisit their former assumptions about law's causes, context, and consequences as well as its potential for social transformation. As subsequent chapters will recount, I make no claim to sophisticated or comprehensive understanding of these phenomena, but they have clearly influenced much of my post-presidential scholarship.

* * *

I began this chapter with a brief account of my family background. I conclude with an even briefer report on how things stand today. I was hugely fortunate in my second marriage, in 1974, to Penny. She is English, a highly respected garden-designer, and someone whose insights about both plants and people are usually pretty accurate. To whatever minimal extent I have avoided the pitfalls of a successful career – workaholism and an inflated view of self – credit is due entirely to her, though she might claim that her best efforts have been in vain. We have two brilliant and successful sons – Joshua, an historian, and Gideon, an arts administrator. They have both managed to flourish in today's rather difficult world and despite the handicap of growing up with a sometimes preoccupied father. They each in turn married a talented and loving woman – Malayna, an education researcher, and Erin, a playwright and actor. But alas, all of them and our four amazing grandchildren – Eli and Carlo, Olive and Tallulah – live too far away to experience our attention and affection on a daily basis.

* * *

This, in brief, is how my life and career have unfolded. What follows are a series of chapters that describe my engagement with history, and with various fields of law, public affairs, or professional activity that have interested me over the years. Or perhaps "describe" is not quite the right word: I make no claim to completeness or even less to objectivity. Rather, I want to convey what I thought I was doing when I immersed myself in these fields, how I understood them and hoped to influence them, and whether and to what extent my fifty-plus years of teaching and writing, administering and recommending have somehow made a difference.

My Encounters with History, Fame, and Celebrity

Of course our lives are shaped to a great extent by the genes we inherit, the families we grow up with, the friends we make, the mentors and colleagues we are fortunate (or, sometimes, unfortunate) enough to encounter. And of course we are influenced by the educations we receive, the books we read, the lessons we learn in the great university of life (or, sometimes, fail to learn). But we cannot deny the great, inexorable, sometimes dispositive force of capital-H History on our lives. Do we grow up, study, make friends, and find work in a time and place characterized by optimism or pessimism, by prosperity or depression, by peace or conflict, by democracy or dictatorship, by egalitarian tendencies or sharp class differences? Not to overstate: History notwithstanding, individuals have some capacity to fashion their own lives. But History is always there; so *there* that sometimes we do not notice it.

I doubt that many members of my own "silent generation" mark the progress of their lives by linking them to the succession of momentous events through which we lived: the Great Depression, World War II, the Holocaust, the Cold War, the American civil rights revolution, the sixties, the brief interlude of postwar social democracy, the triumph of globalization and neo-liberalism, the fall of Soviet communism and the rise of China, the transformation of personal relationships, and the digital revolution. But I do. Perhaps this is because my family was interested in politics, perhaps because I was particularly fortunate in the teachers I encountered, perhaps because my own professional and intellectual interests made me more aware of historical developments than most. Or perhaps my chance encounters with History have helped me retain memories that I might otherwise have lost.

I don't want to over-promise. Those encounters were relatively innocuous, not to say anticlimactic. However, they did take place in the first person singular and consequently left me with the sense that I participated in some way in the great events of my times.

For my generation, "History" was the looming world war that shaped our consciousness as children. Growing up in Canada during the war, I was spared the terror and the misery that haunted my contemporaries elsewhere. But "the war" was what we played at, what we listened to on the radio, what darkened the lives of neighbours and schoolmates who lost family members, what our high school teachers – many of them traumatized veterans – brought back into their classrooms.

Although the excruciating details of the Holocaust emerged only after the war and didn't become part of a widely accepted narrative until the late 1950s, like most Jewish children, I had heard tales of prejudice, persecution, and pogroms for as long as I can remember. No thanks to my formal Jewish education, of which I had very little: rather, my historical consciousness was shaped by stories that emerged from my grandmother's work with immigrants, refugees, and relief organizations, through media reportage, and in response to the Jewish community's efforts to ensure that "never again" would the world allow genocide to occur. The high-point of those efforts was the kidnapping, trial, and execution by the State of Israel of Adolf Eichmann, a Nazi functionary with significant responsibility for transporting Jews to their death. I happened to be in Israel in the spring of 1961 when the Eichmann trial began, and was able to attend it for two days. There he was, a sharp-featured, thin man in a glass booth, listening to the charges being read, pleading "*nicht schuldig*" (not guilty) to each. And there they were, scores of survivors and relatives of those who did not survive, sobbing and fulminating, outraged and overcome with grief. I will never forget this encounter with one of History's greatest crimes, nor will I deny my ambivalence about the legally ambiguous events that made the trial possible and its outcome inevitable.

World War II gave way to the Cold War, and for a terrible moment during the Cuban missile crisis of 1962, it appeared that the cold war might degenerate into thermonuclear conflict. The triggering event was the threat by the Soviet Union to install nuclear weapons in Cuba to protect its ally, the fledgling Communist regime led by Fidel Castro. However, when I had my personal Castro moment, in the spring of 1959, no such conflict was in prospect. Having seized power in Cuba on 1 January of that year, Castro had not yet revealed himself as a communist. Indeed, within a few months he had launched a charm offensive on American university campuses, including Harvard, where I was studying. And a well-choreographed offensive it was too. Here is the scene: a grassy slope behind the university's football stadium; 10,000 students excitedly awaiting this charismatic figure; sunset on a warm April evening. A motorcade of fish-tailed Cadillac convertibles roars up. Castro – tall, tanned, bearded, kinetic – vaults over the side of his car and races up the stairs to a floodlit balcony. He flings his arms wide and embraces the crowd. "Jews of America!" he shouts. Astonishment. A collective intake of breath. Then gradually we decipher the message: "Youth of America" is what he was saying. Castro spoke for an hour or so – mostly about baseball, as I recall. This was a very different Castro from the one who seemed about to provoke a nuclear war during the missile crisis of 1962.

My second encounter with the Cold War occurred in 1963. After a vacation in Yugoslavia and Bulgaria, I received a plain brown envelope containing an invitation from a Canadian intelligence agency called the Defence Research Board to tell them about my trip. The temptation was irresistible. Arrangements for a rendezvous were made in the best cloak-and-dagger fashion: a postcard, a phone call at a pre-arranged hour, a room in a midtown Toronto hotel, a code name. During the course of my day-long de-briefing, I was able to draw on my strong visual memory to recount that chocolate bars were on sale in my hotel in Sofia, that a certain railway crossing barrier was still operated manually by the old woman in a red kerchief, and that East German tourists were numerous at the Slanchev Bryag resort where I had stayed. Having shared this valuable information with our NATO allies, I abandoned my career in espionage – but not before asking my handler why I hadn't been asked in advance to keep my eyes open for whatever it was his organization was looking for. "We don't tell people," he explained, "because they might get themselves in trouble."

No one who came of age watching television during the 1950s and 1960s could be unaware of America's great civil rights revolution. However, my own encounters with that revolution were not entirely confined to television. In September 1957, just before starting our final year of law school, I hitchhiked to Mexico with my friend Martin Friedland.[1] On our way south we passed through Meridian, Mississippi, where just two years earlier a black teenager, Emmett Till, had been murdered for allegedly flirting with a white woman. The national outrage this murder triggered and the local climate of fear were both dramatized for us by a chance encounter with a hitch-hiking black soldier *en route* to his family's farm not far away. On our way back north, we heard radio reports of the drama being played out in Little Rock, Arkansas, where efforts were under way to desegregate the local high school. We detoured to Little Rock, claimed to represent the Canadian University Press, and met some journalists from one of the US television networks. They provided us with a car and cameraman and sent us in search of the son of the segregationist governor, Orville Faubus, who was rumoured to be attending an integrated college in the north of the state. Dodging the state police who (we imagined) were hot on our trail, we failed to find Faubus Jr, but managed to film his dorm room decorated with Confederate flags. Or so we thought: alas, our anxious cameraman had forgotten to remove the lens cap on his camera.

My next direct encounter with the struggle for America's soul came ten years later, in 1967, when I was conducting a human rights enquiry in Windsor. As I found my way to the courthouse where the hearing was being held, the smoke was still rising from the terrible race riots which a few days earlier had destroyed much of downtown Detroit. The genial policeman who was providing security at my hearing gestured across the river and assured me that if he had a tank, he would go over there and "fix those f***ing n****rs." Racism, it seems, acknowledges neither shame nor national boundaries. Or to put the same thought differently, Canadians had (and have) no reason to feel smug about being a more just society than the US or having escaped the civil strife across the border.

Personal holidays and professional travel have led to many other encounters with History. I will mention just three. In 1974, Penny and I were on our honeymoon on the small Aegean island of Skiathos. We noticed a lot of overflying military aircraft which, it turned out, had been scrambled because of a *coup d'état* in Cyprus. By good luck, we boarded one of the last flights to leave Athens airport before it was closed for several days during the ensuing crisis, which ended with the Turkish invasion of the island and the downfall of

Greece's ruling military junta. We were in the Soviet Union in 1988 at the height of *glasnost* and witnessed the first spontaneous popular demonstrations to take place in Tbilisi, Georgia, for seventy years. And later that same year, I gave a lecture on administrative law at Beijing University to a classroom full of Communist *cadres* who had been sent back to school to learn about the rule of law. The blood-bath in Tiananmen Square six months later suggests that my lecture was not entirely successful.

History was shaping my life; but my sporadic and accidental encounters with it – as I came to realize – shaped History not at all. I might have been intimidated by this realization, might have abandoned my commitment to making the world a better place. Fortunately, my sense of irony has allowed me to live fairly comfortably with the contradiction between my large ambition and my very limited capacity to change the course of events.

So much for History. What about celebrity and fame? I do not have much time for people who are famous for being famous. However, I have great regard for people who have contributed to scholarship, to progressive causes, and to my own education.

As a law student, professor, and dean, I met many distinguished jurists and public officials in the line of duty. While I cannot claim intimate acquaintance with any of them, in one or two cases their biographers awarded me a place in their footnotes.[2] When I became president of York University, the range of these encounters broadened. York had an admirable tradition of awarding honorary degrees *in absentia* to distinguished prisoners of conscience. When their incarceration ended, and they were able to collect their degrees in person, it occasionally fell to me to deliver the documents attesting to their honour. Thus, following his release from Robben Island in 1990, I was able to greet Nelson Mandela during his tour of North America, before 30,000 enthusiastic supporters in front of the Ontario legislature, and to deliver a diploma to Vaclav Havel before an ecstatic audience of Czechoslovak-Canadians at Convocation Hall at the University of Toronto. York also conferred honorary degrees on several heads of state, enabling me to briefly meet presidents Chaim Herzog of Israel, François Mitterand of France, and Francesco Cossiga of Italy. These latter encounters left me with an enhanced appreciation of what it must mean to live under a dense security blanket. It also left me a bit apprehensive about what might happen to someone (me!) who chanced to be standing next to a president when security failed.

Not surprisingly, many of those who qualify for entry into my personal Pantheon were labour lawyers. I have already mentioned my mentors, Bora Laskin and Sydney Robins. I was also fortunate enough early on to encounter Otto Kahn-Freund, an emigré Weimar labour judge, who is often identified as "the father of British labour law." He edited the journal in which I published my early study on Danish labour lore and labour law, and sent me a congratulatory note which led to a sporadic correspondence and long-distance friendship that lasted over two decades. It ended when I received an offprint of something he had written, apparently mailed to me the day before he died. A memorable moment in that friendship occurred in 1975, when Kahn-Freund received an honorary doctorate from York University and I was able to introduce him to my ten-day-old son, Joshua. Bill (later Lord Bill) Wedderburn was a leading English labour scholar who introduced the subject to the Cambridge law curriculum in the early 1960s and subsequently held a chair at the LSE. We met when I invited him to a labour law conference – his first visit to North America. However, in our family he is famous not just for his prolific, learned, and influential scholarship, and his passionate advocacy of labour's cause in academic circles and in the House of Lords, but – more importantly – for introducing me to Penny at a dinner party at his home in North London. Bob Hepple, an activist lawyer in South Africa, had represented Nelson Mandela and been scooped up with other anti-apartheid activists; he escaped from prison and found his way to England where he pursued a distinguished career as a labour lawyer, tribunal chair, and academic. Bob was one of my hosts during my sabbatical sojourn at Clare Hall, Cambridge, in 1971, and remained a life-long friend. He and I were honoured in 2013 as the first recipients of lifetime achievement awards from the newly-founded Labour Law Research Network, an award that now bears his name.

In the United States, as I have mentioned, I was taught by Archibald Cox, a senior figure in the field, and by Derek Bok, then in his first year of teaching. Cox was impressive but unhelpful. He tried to dissuade me from enrolling in his advanced labour law seminar, on the grounds that the previous year a Japanese student had done so and fared poorly. I persisted, and he agreed to take me on. My fellow students included Michael Dukakis (future governor of Massachusetts and failed 1988 Democratic presidential candidate) and Carl Levin (later a long-serving Democratic senator from Michigan). It was in this seminar that I first encountered the ideas that led to my influential 1965 article, "The Dependent Contractor: A Study of the Legal Problems of Countervailing Power."[3] If Cox was unwelcoming, Bok was the opposite, a stimulating and engaged teacher. One day his father – a prominent judge – came to see his son teach a labour law class. As it happened, the third-year members of the class had attended their graduation banquet the previous evening and brilliant as they were, they were too hung over to contribute to the discussion. I wasn't, however, and I did, thus sparing Bok the embarrassment of having to explain the apparent apathy of his students to his father. Almost thirty years later, when he was president of Harvard, Bok returned the favour by participating in the symposium I organized to mark York's twenty-fifth anniversary and the beginning of my presidency.

Another American labour lawyer was also influential in my early career. Robert Mathews, a founding member of the Labour Law Group, invited me to join it in the mid-1960s. The Group had essentially reinvented the subject at a weeklong seminar in Ann Arbor in 1947. It had appointed Mathews as the senior editor of an innovative casebook built around the ongoing narrative of union-management relations in the fictitious "Enderby Rubber Company." This narrative generated legal problems which students were invited to resolve; to open their minds, they were also confronted with ethical dilemmas arising from the practice of labour law and with international and comparative materials. Even more unusually, the casebook project was not only genuinely collaborative but idealistic as well. Members of the Group agreed to hold all profits from the casebook in trust to support education in labour law. And most astonishingly, the Group has renewed itself and remains active seventy years on. I expressed my gratitude for Mathews's invitation by establishing a Canadian counterpart, which published its first casebook in the late 1960s and is still going strong today. Mathews also persuaded me to launch a course on the legal profession, another of his interests; I became the first Canadian academic to teach the subject. And finally, he introduced me to the system of informal dispute resolution that had grown up in the isolated and then-lawyerless village of Monson, Maine, where his family had had a home since the early nineteenth century. (His grandfather was Thoreau's stage coach driver.) This was an early and provocative encounter with what I came later to know as "legal pluralism."

I would like to claim that my own most famous students owe all their success to my courses in labour law. This would clearly be untrue, but I am proud to have had as students and/or research assistants such distinguished labour academics as Paul Weiler (the first Canadian appointed to Harvard's law faculty), Judy Fudge (McMaster), Pierre Verge (dean of law at Laval University), David Beatty (University of Toronto), David Doorey (York University), and Claire Mummé (University of Windsor), as well as countless local legal luminaries including justices Warren Winkler (chief justice of Ontario) and George Adams, and leading practitioners such as Don Brown, Paul Cavalluzzo, and Chris Paliare. And I equally value the opportunities I have had to work with labour law colleagues at other universities, such as Brian Langille and Kerry Rittich (Toronto), Innis Christie (Dalhousie), Bernie Adell (Queen's), Gilles Trudeau (Montréal), Mark Freedland and Hugh Collins (Oxford), Kathy Stone (UCLA), Matt Finkin (Illinois), David Trubek (Wisconsin), Cindy Estlund (NYU), and Karl Klare (Northeastern).

At some point early in my career, during the 1960s, I sensed that if I was to make my mark, I would have to stop "thinking like a lawyer" and adopt broader perspectives on the social and political issues that law sought – usually unsuccessfully – to address. My first interdisciplinary partner was John Crispo, founding director of the University of Toronto's Centre for Industrial Relations. Crispo later developed a reputation as a controversialist with libertarian leanings. However, he was smart, funny, and open-minded, and offered me my initial experience of working with someone who had an intellectual frame of reference quite different from my own. At about the same time I met Hans Mohr, a scholar with extraordinary reach. Trained as a philologist in Austria, he became a social worker in rural Saskatchewan, then a researcher at the Clarke Institute of Psychiatry and ultimately, at my instance, a member of the Osgoode faculty with a cross appointment in sociology. He later served as a member of the Law Reform Commission of Canada. Hans read everything – philosophy, law, history, psychology; he read in several languages; he was interested in literature, music, and art; he was an accomplished handyman and later in life moved to a farm near Kingston. Hans generously read drafts of virtually everything I wrote and provided both encouragement and much-needed critique.

Another constant correspondent and friendly critic was Rod Macdonald, sometime dean of the McGill law faculty, chair of the

Law Commission of Canada, and president of the Royal Society of Canada. He too had extraordinarily broad interests, utterly refused to recognize the borders between academic disciplines, and was hugely generous to his friends, colleagues, and students whom he treated with admirable democratic disregard for rank or reputation.[4] And finally, I was lucky during my post-presidential career to fall in with Daniel Drache, a talented professor of political economy whose position as head of York's Robarts Centre for Canadian Studies enabled him to engage leading scholars around the world in spirited debates on topics as diverse as "regulation," "cultural flows," "defiant publics," theories of economic development, and Canadian public policy. He generously invited me to participate in some of these debates, which have taken me to the far corners of the globe and of the world of the intellect.

However, my most sustained and intense interdisciplinary collaboration, as it turns out, arrived towards the very end of my academic career. I was first an advisor to, and then an active participant in, a remarkable international, interdisciplinary consortium called CRIMT – Centre de Recherche Interuniversitaire sur la Mondialisation et le Travail. Its organizing genius, Gregor Murray from the Université de Montréal, has accomplished one of the most difficult feats imaginable: he has enabled scores of individualistic researchers and practitioners speaking different languages, in different disciplinary and ideological vernaculars, from different countries and continents, to engage in a fifteen-year-long conversation that has left us all not only wiser but wanting more.

So what have these fortuitous brushes with History meant, these fleeting encounters and close engagements with historic events, colourful personalities, and great minds? I wish I could say that they made me into a first-rate scholar and influential public intellectual. However, while I think I've done a decent job at most things I've turned my hand to, I haven't been a stellar performer in any of my endeavours. "Not so," people may say, if they read my c.v.; "You're very distinguished." And indeed, I have amassed a tasteful collection of honorary doctorates, lifetime achievement awards, honorific fellowships, and government gongs. However, I am only prepared to describe my career as "distinguished" if the adjective is accompanied by quotation marks whenever it goes out for a stroll.

The truth is that I owe my "distinction" primarily to being in the right place at the right time. As I often claim, deciding where and when to be born is the most important decision one can make. I wisely decided on Toronto in 1935 – a member of the small generation sometimes known as "the lucky few." This ensured that I was out of harm's way during the war; that the anti-semitism I experienced personally was mostly mindless and mild rather than vicious and deadly; that I was a university student through the relatively optimistic period of postwar recovery rather than during the Great Depression; that my academic career began just as universities were expanding and restructuring to accommodate the great wave of baby boomers; and that I hit my stride professionally in the 1960s in an era when law and legal education, industrial relations, and politics were all opening up to new ideas and new people. Forty or fifty years on, as institutions and movements launched in the sixties came to maturity, as they began to manufacture their own traditions and construct their own pantheons, my generation of doers and thinkers was of an age to be treated as totemic. It is no coincidence that I have been the first recipient of no less than three newly established lifetime contribution awards (two for labour law and one for the social sciences).

Longevity helps as well. It will soon be sixty years since my first article was published in the *Canadian Bar Review*. My first graduate student retired several years ago after serving twenty years on the bench. I've taught and worked with the children and grandchildren of people whom I had taught or worked with at the beginning and middle of my career. Nonetheless, my phone still rings occasionally and not all of my email is spam. From time to time I'm asked to address a class, a colloquium, or a conference; my advice is occasionally sought by governments (which is not to say that it is necessarily followed); and once or twice a year, I'll publish something that – a point of principle – constitutes a new departure in my thinking or a new focus for my scholarship. I hope I'm not famous for being famous, but I happily acknowledge the essential truth of the aphorism attributed to Woody Allen (himself born in 1935): "Eighty percent of success is just showing up." He and I have both been showing up for a very long time.

3

Labour Law – My Subject, My Passion

In chapter 1, I described how a combination of family history, academic encounters, and intellectual interests led me to choose labour law as the primary focus of my career. There was much to recommend that choice. Labour law was interesting because it straddled the traditional boundary between public and private law; it invited interdisciplinary analysis and was the subject of spirited policy debates; and it mattered: it affected the lives of millions of workers, shaped the success of our economy, and was a major proving ground for Canada's claim to be a just and democratic nation. Moreover, during the 1950s and 1960s, labour law was just coming into its own as an academic subject.[1] Indeed, as things turned out, specializing in labour law was a very good career move. By the mid-1960s, within a few years of my entering academe – during which Bora Laskin and several other prominent scholars departed the field – I was arguably the most senior and high-profile labour law professor in Canada.

Obviously, I did not invent myself as a labour scholar. I am very much in debt to my mentor, Laskin, and was deeply influenced as a graduate student at Harvard by my courses in US labour law taught, as I've mentioned, by Archibald Cox and Derek Bok. This made for occasional moments of embarrassment. While at Harvard, I returned to Toronto for a visit and went to see Laskin at my *alma mater*. To my surprise, he invited me to come to his labour law class to share my thoughts on how studying the subject at Harvard differed from the experience his students were having. I blush to recall that I ungraciously praised Harvard for its closer engagement with the real world of industrial relations and its deeper exploration of the social and political dimension of labour law issues. However, Laskin took my remarks in good spirit, and when he left teaching to join the Ontario Court of Appeal in 1965, he asked me to commute from Osgoode to teach his course at Toronto as well.

One of the oddities of academic law in the 1960s (and for some decades thereafter) was that scholars made their reputations by publishing collections of teaching materials – casebooks – rather than treatises, textbooks, or monographs. This preoccupation was both the cause and the consequence of two closely linked historical deficiencies in Canadian law: too few full-time scholars and too meagre a corpus of scholarly literature. On the other hand, it gave me and my academic contemporaries the opportunity to invent or re-invent our subjects, to create new taxonomies and tropes, to deconstruct old clichés and categories. By educating successive generations of students to see things differently, we naively felt we would ultimately influence the way our particular field of law was perceived and practised.[2] Nowhere did this prospect seem more promising than in newly developed fields such as labour law, where economic structures, public policy, and legal regimes all seemed to be evolving rapidly and in a progressive direction.[3] In my first few years of teaching I duly produced my own casebook, based partly on Laskin's teaching materials, partly on Cox and Bok's. Then in the late 1960s, inspired by the example of the American Labour Law Group mentioned in chapter 2,[4] I brought together four or five of my fellow labour academics to collaborate in the development of an innovative casebook for use across Canada. Eight editions and five decades later, our Canadian group – its membership constantly renewed – continues to rethink labour and employment law. But, as might have been predicted, we founding editors over-estimated the ability of law professors to change the law by changing the way we taught it.

Perhaps sensing the limits of this approach to the reinvention of labour law, I embarked on what was then seen as an ambitious program of scholarly publication (on average, two articles a year through the 1960s). Like many novice academics then and now, I launched my publishing career by revising a paper that I had written at graduate school. The title was "Tort Liability for Strikes in Canada," but the subtitle says it all: "Some Problems of Judicial Workmanship."[5] A similar perspective informed my contributions to the spirited academic and professional debates of the mid-1960s around the willingness of courts to grant injunctions against union strikes and picketing. Judges ("with respect," as we used to say, meaning the contrary) had twisted the law out of shape and transgressed basic principles of procedural fairness in their eagerness to protect employer interests.[6] But it could be otherwise, I maintained. If only judges were more rigorous in their reasoning, and more sensitive to the realities of labour relations, they could do much to reconfigure labour law so that it was better suited to contemporary needs.

Yet I suppose I harboured doubts even then about the prospects for a judicial *volte-face*. On the one hand, I argued for legislation that would eliminate, reduce, or reform the common law of industrial conflict and indeed, in the end, a combination of judicial and legislative initiatives accomplished just that. On the other, in a series of articles over the next decade, I gradually convinced myself (but very few others) that "labour lore" – the informal "law of the shop" that emerges in every workplace – could, should, and did in fact displace state "labour law" in whole or in part. I never managed to integrate these two lines of argument, but nonetheless held firmly to the view that the scope of labour law ought to be determined by the policy logic of "countervailing power," not by the juridical logic of Victorian "master and servant" law.

My contributions to policy logic and to the reform of labour law were not confined to the pages of law reviews. Early on, I was appointed to assist two government enquiries, one concerned with the appointment of labour arbitrators, the other with the promotion of safer workplaces. Then I undertook a major study of public-interest labour disputes[7] for the Woods Task Force on Labour Relations, whose landmark report recommended important reforms in Canada's laws. And throughout the sixties, I made several clandestine contributions to policy development as a result of my relationship with Jacob Finkelman, one of Canada's first labour law scholars, the founding and long-serving chair of the Ontario Labour Relations Board. The Labour Ministry frequently called upon Finkelman for advice on legislative policy and drafting, and he, in turn, sometimes asked me to consult informally with him. Perhaps my most significant clandestine contribution was to persuade him that "dependent contractors" should be deemed "employees" under the Labour Relations Act, thus permitting the owner-operators of trucks and taxi cabs to bargain collectively with their *de facto* employers. As enacted some years later, the language of the statute closely tracked my own proposal.[8]

In 1967, Finkelman moved to Ottawa to become the founding chair of the federal Public Service Staff Relations Board. He persuaded me to head up its grievance adjudication system, and I spent a year or so commuting to Ottawa where I not only heard and decided cases but designed and administered the new regime and recruited the initial cohort of adjudicators. When he left for Ottawa, Finkelman arranged for me to succeed him as chair of both the men's and women's garment industry in Toronto, posts he had occupied since 1937. These chairmanships had been established in 1920, long before grievance arbitration became commonplace (and ultimately compulsory) in other sectors, and the system provided cheap, speedy, informal, and user-friendly dispute-resolution to unions and employers. I did my best not only to respond to the traditions and needs of the industry, but to advertise the experience of the garment industry chairmanship as a shining example of how grievance arbitration systems more generally ought to function. It was, in fact, a practical demonstration of why "lore" often served the parties better than "law."

My appointments as an arbitrator in the garment industry and the federal public service were by no means my first. Through the 1960s, I had served as chair of conciliation boards or as a mediator on perhaps a dozen occasions and had also chaired boards of inquiry into human rights complaints. More significantly, I began arbitrating in 1962, and within ten years had decided about one hundred cases. Many of my decisions involved mill-run disputes about discharge or discipline, work assignments, or contract interpretation, and while I hoped and believed that my approach to grievance arbitration was an improvement on the state of the art, I had few illusions about its influence on labour law and policy in general. However, several of my decisions were more consequential. In *Welland County General Hospital*[9] – the first case decided under legislation requiring that bargaining disputes in hospitals be settled by arbitration – I laid down a series of arbitral principles that continue to be used today. The following year I decided *Russelsteel*, a case that today is universally (if wrongly) read as establishing that employers have the right to contract out work unless they agree not to.[10] However, by far the most important decision I made during this period was *Port Arthur Shipbuilding*, in which I explicitly rejected the notion that arbitrators were obliged to apply the common law of contract when deciding cases under a collective agreement. Freed from that constraint, I ruled, they could do what common law judges could not: they could substitute a lesser penalty for the one imposed by an employer on a misbehaving employee. This was not a radical move: I was simply doing what most arbitrators had been doing for years. Alas, this fact that did not impress the Supreme Court of Canada; it peremptorily overturned my decision.[11] Nonetheless, my view prevailed in the end. I organized a letter, signed by virtually all Ontario labour arbitrators, that ultimately persuaded the minister of labour to amend the legislation so as to restore the remedial power we thought we already had.

The Supreme Court's *Port Arthur* decision, and several others decided at about the same time and with similar disregard for industrial relations realities and the evolving "law of the shop," confirmed my long-standing belief that courts had no business meddling in labour law – a belief that launched me on an academic project that was to last, one way or another, for the next forty years. It also left me with a declining appetite for involvement in the arbitration process.

Nonetheless, my career as an arbitrator stuttered on, focused mostly on my role as chair of the garment industry, until another disappointing judicial decision finally brought it to an end. As mentioned, arbitration in the garment industry began in 1920. From that time down to the 1980s, so far as the records disclosed, no lawyer had ever appeared to argue a case on behalf of either employers or unions. Indeed, there was little a lawyer could have contributed. There were no witnesses: the chair elicited the facts by questioning the spokespersons from each side. There was no reference to formal rules of law: the parties regarded themselves as bound by their agreement and by long-standing customs which were sometimes recorded in a small notebook but often conjured up out of their shared memory of local lore and practice. There was no recourse to conventional legal remedies: the parties did what the chair directed them to do to make things right.

This blissful, extra-legal regime depended on the desire of labour and management to conduct their relationship without recourse to formal law. However, after some sixty years, that desire was fading and in 1979, the dominant firm in the industry decided to break with tradition and brought in a lawyer to argue its case. I refused to allow him to do so but he persuaded the Court of Appeal to set aside my ruling and, in due course, lengthy, costly, and contentious arbitration proceedings ensued which proved how wise the parties had been in forgoing the assistance of lawyers for the preceding six decades.[12]

Essentially, this episode marked the beginning of the end for the garment industry's unique arbitration system. Combined with other unpleasant developments in the field – increasing legalism, intensified partisanship[13] – it also marked the beginning of the end of my desire to serve as an arbitrator.

I heard my last case in 1984, just before becoming president of York University. However, my experience as a mediator and arbitrator left me with a skill set that proved to be valuable in both university administration and later, public policy consulting work. More importantly, it informed my academic work on legal pluralism, which began in the 1960s and continues to be a significant focus of my research. Labour law, I argued, was not like other fields of law. Indeed, much of it had emerged as a reaction to the failure of the mainstream legal system to deal fairly or effectively with labour-management relations. Most substantive rules of labour law differed from those of the common law and often originated in agreements, implicit understandings, and patterns of behaviour developed by the immediate parties or the broader labour-management community; disputes were mostly decided by specialized tribunals, often deploying distinctive procedures and remedies, and with the participation of lay advocates and decision-makers; and the use of "countervailing power" was accepted as legitimate and necessary. Given these unique characteristics, I argued, labour law was emerging as a semi-autonomous legal regime in which workers would enjoy "industrial citizenship" – an array of unique rights that defined their relationship to employers and the state.[14]

This argument was part description, part advocacy, part wishful thinking – and wholly anathema to most jurists. I elaborated on the "citizenship" theme and on the autonomy of labour law in subsequent publications,[15] but the concept never gained much traction outside academic circles.[16] If anything, practitioners and judges (and some labour scholars) have been arguing for the tighter integration of labour law into the general legal system, especially with a view to ensuring Charter protection for the rights of workers and unions. Good luck to them: three decades of Charter protections have coincided with steady declines in union membership, militancy, and power, in labour's share of the GDP, and in social and economic equality more generally.[17]

In 1985, my career in labour law took an odd turn. As president of York, I became an employer. In that capacity, I had to deal occasionally

with difficult and/or troubled employees and hyper-aggressive manag-
ers, with bad faith, perversity, and plain foolishness. More often, I was
confronted with genuine naiveté, justifiable indignation, and principled obstructionism. But mostly I just encountered people acting in
their own interests, asserting what they honestly believed to be their
rights, while framing their arguments in ways that generally appealed
to some plausible version of the "true values" of the university and
Canadian society. None of this surprised me. What did was how difficult it was to reconcile the traditions and structures of university
governance with labour law and policy. Faculty members wearing
their union hats sought higher salaries; wearing their hats as members
of senate or as departmental chairs, they wanted to spend the same
dollars to hire more professors or improve the library. Promotion and
tenure standards and procedures are critical to the ethos of excellence
that is central to any university's mission, and were therefore within
the jurisdiction of our academic senate; however, they are also "terms
and conditions of employment" whose determination is consigned
by law to the collective bargaining process. Many senior academic
administrators come from the ranks of the professoriate and return
there when they finish their term as presidents, vice-presidents, or
deans; but the Labour Relations Act contemplates an arm's length,
adversarial relationship between management and labour – even if
they are former and future friends and colleagues. I had to acknowledge these contradictions and find practical ways to navigate around
them, but I never resolved them.

As a labour law scholar, then, I took away two insights from
my experience as president. First, it isn't easy being an employer
– especially an employer with good intentions. People are difficult;
resources are limited; conflicts of interest and ideology may be miti-
gated by good will but they persist nonetheless; and to a large extent,
problems within any given employment relationship are inevitably
intertwined with difficulties in the wider world that can't be cured
and must therefore be endured. Second, every workplace is unique:
universities aren't like automobile factories or railways; they aren't
even much like each other. One size of labour relations system doesn't
fit all. However, it was developments in political economy, not my
presidential experiences, that shaped the next phase of my career as
a labour scholar – by far the most productive and interesting.

My 1985 article on industrial pluralism,[18] the last piece I wrote
before becoming president of York, represented the high-water mark

of my effort to understand labour law from the perspective of legal pluralism, a socio-legal theory that I describe in some detail in chapter 10. In this article I argued (persuasively, I thought) that quotidian work routines and patterns of interpersonal relations – not formal legal rules – constituted the effective law of the workplace. However, events in the 1980s and 1990s persuaded me that if this had once been true, it no longer was. It became increasingly (if belatedly) clear to me that the shelf life of the postwar social contract had expired and with it, the system of workplace relations it embodied. Canada, like so many other countries, had experienced what I called "globalization of the mind":[19] many of its leading intellectuals and policy-makers, its editorial writers and politicians, had become committed to neo-liberalism. The implications for labour law and policy, and for the theory and practice of industrial relations, were profound.

Power lay at the heart of the problem. Collective bargaining, a central pillar of Canada's labour policy since the mid-1940s, was in effect a strategy of countervailing power. By enabling workers to bargain through unions and requiring employers to negotiate with them in good faith, we thought we would create a situation in which both parties would share responsibility for establishing and administering the law of the workplace. This, I argued in an early article, would ensure that workers became "industrial citizens" – that they would enjoy in the context of employment the rights that we all aspired to as citizens of the broader polity.[20] But in retrospect, it is clear that I had underestimated the extent to which workplace norms were – like state law – shaped by relations of unequal power. By the time I returned to my scholarly work, after seven-plus years as president, the advent of globalization, the turn to neo-liberalism, and the resulting trauma of the "new economy" had made the issue of unequal power impossible to ignore.[21]

Moreover, in my earlier work I had failed to appreciate how much the welfare state had facilitated the collective bargaining system by shifting primary responsibility for the provision of health care, pensions, unemployment insurance, and job training from the "social partners" to the state. As the welfare state fell into disrepute and disrepair – partly because taxpayers (including union members) no longer wished to pay for it – the industrial relations system experienced additional stress. But most of all, I had not understood how much the so-called Wagner Act model of collective bargaining that Canada had imported from the United States was a product of its time and place. That system was designed primarily for semi-skilled industrial workers, but these workers were now being displaced by new technologies. It operated against a background expectation that governments would strive to maintain full employment, but globalization had made it increasingly difficult for them to manage their labour markets. It assumed that firms would become ever more vertically and horizontally integrated, thus creating relatively stable internal labour markets for their employees, but new management strategies led firms instead to seek "flexibility" by developing lengthy, often trans-national, supply and marketing chains, and to shrink their "core" labour force or do away with it altogether. Most importantly, the Wagner model had been introduced during the Great Depression in the United States and during World War II in Canada. This was an era when labour's increasing political and industrial militancy made it expedient for both governments and employers to embrace relatively benign and orderly regimes of labour market regulation. But from the 1970s onwards, with the decline of labour solidarity, militancy, and power, the calculus of expediency began to change.

An article I published a few years after my return to academic life, "Labour Law without the State,"[22] represented my first effort to provide a comprehensive account of how these developments (which I called "the new economy") were threatening the postwar system of industrial relations and labour law – the system I had studied, had worked in, and at the margins, had helped to design, build, and manage. In its own terms, this effort was fairly successful. However, it left a difficult question unresolved: how to square this account of the damage wrought by the external forces of the new economy with my longstanding contention that labour law is an autonomous system shaped largely by internal forces. A second essay, "Landscape and Memory," offered a possible answer in the form of what I called "critical legal pluralism": "power relations [are] a major determinant of all legal regimes of employment whether originating in the state, the workplace or elsewhere."[23]

As time went on, I became increasingly interested in why and how and with what consequences power – "a major determinant of all legal regimes" – was shifting away from labour. This led me to a series of increasingly pessimistic reflections concerning the potential of our present system of labour law to survive the impact of technology, new managerial strategies, globalization, and neo-liberalism.[24]

My pessimism, ultimately, led me to this conclusion: union density was falling, union industrial strength was ebbing, and union political influence was dwindling because working class culture, identity, and solidarity were dissolving. What, I asked myself, could possibly be the future of labour law "after labour"?[25]

Friends and colleagues urged me to adopt a more optimistic outlook, and I tried earnestly to do so. Would the dispersal of production around the world, I wondered, empower unions by creating new pressure points?[26] Would employers come to realize that treating workers decently was good for business?[27] Might strong informal normative systems emerge within corporations to replace the decaying statutory regime?[28] Would governments faced with social or economic crises conclude that they could only save capitalism by reforming it, much as they did in the 1930s?[29] I even briefly entertained the thought – such was the extremity of my despair – that collective bargaining might be saved by the unexpected Supreme Court rulings, from about 2000 onwards, that interpreted the Charter as guaranteeing workers the freedom to organize, negotiate, strike, and picket.[30]

All to no avail. I could not see that any of these developments was likely to halt the decline of the labour law system to which I had devoted much of my professional career. As a last resort, I turned to a form of historical magic: I conjured up a counter-factual. Suppose, I supposed, that labour law had not been invented as an academic discipline and field of legal practice in response to the tumultuous political and economic events of 1920s and 1930s. Suppose instead that its architects had seen employment not as a distinct category of juridical relations but as one of many in which the subordinate party sought to resist the stronger by economic, social, and legal means?[31] Of course, *The Law of Economic Subordination and Resistance* never did emerge in the 1930s, but (for reasons I cited) it might well have. Had it done so, many shortcomings of labour law might have been avoided; the field might have been less vulnerable to developments that subsequently brought it to the brink of extinction; technologies of resistance pioneered in the labour field might have been deployed to protect other subordinated groups; and such groups might have formed common cause with workers to secure legislation that entrenched general principles of social justice for the benefit of all powerless people. "Might have" but didn't: that's the nature of historical counter-factuals.

In a companion piece delivered, perhaps inappropriately, to the fiftieth-anniversary celebrations of the Canadian Industrial Relations Research Association, I suggested that their field of study, no less than my own, had described a similar trajectory, rising to an optimistic and influential high through the 1960s, then subsiding to its present pessimistic and marginal low. How to regain its momentum, how to address current realities? Here is what I proposed: "there will come a moment when we have all had enough of unstable markets, lopsided power relations, widespread unfairness and declining living standards. When that moment arrives, IR scholars who have enrolled in the new discipline of economic power and resistance will become very influential indeed – and useful as well."[32] My counter-factual, like a benign version of Frankenstein's monster, seems to have escaped from my scholarly imaginary and, at least for now, has me in its grip.

4

Public Law – 'Tis Better to Have Loved and Lost

When I began my academic career, I was assured that I would be assigned to teach constitutional law. Somehow, that assignment never came my way. After I became dean and had an opportunity to peruse my own personnel file, I learned why: Osgoode's senior public-law scholar had persuaded our then-dean that my views on the constitution had been unduly influenced by my mentor (and his intellectual adversary), Laskin, and that they were so unsound that I should never be allowed to inflict them on students. And I never was. Instead, I was assigned to "assist" that same faculty member in his course on administrative law. It was never clear whether my views on the latter subject were considered less unsound or whether it was thought that my designation as his "assistant" would send a signal to students to disregard my heretical ideas. In any event, after a year in this supporting role, I was allowed to teach administrative law on my own. As it turned out, from my colleague's point of view, I probably shouldn't have been.

In my file, alongside the note recommending my lifetime ban from the sacred precincts of the constitution, was a memo from the dean recording with distaste something I had apparently said (though I cannot remember where or when). The purpose of public law, I had opined, is not just to protect citizens from abuses by the government; it is also to enable the government to protect citizens from abuses of private power. This position was no doubt influenced by my immersion in labour law; after all, its *raison d'etre* is to protect vulnerable workers from powerful employers. However, if charged with constitutional heresy, I would have had to plead guilty. I believed then that the most important function of public law is to enable the state to promote the public interest – to regulate financial markets, protect the environment, ensure fair treatment for consumers, and provide social goods such as public education and health care. My views haven't changed much in the interim. In 1981, as a member of the Economic Council of Canada, I dissented from its report recommending extensive deregulation of the national economy[1] – so far as I know, the only dissent in the Council's history. And I would say pretty much the same today.

At any rate, when I was just starting out, my position was anathema to those jurists who, like my senior colleague, believed that the mission of public law was to promote the rule of law, a principle that required judges not only to serve as custodians of legality and guarantors of individual freedoms but also to defend the polity against the perceived excesses of interventionist governments. Courts can perform this latter function (they believe) by reviewing, and if necessary overturning, decisions of state officials and regulatory agencies that do not conform to law. My view differs somewhat. Governments that do nothing are seldom reviewed, and those that promote the interests of the rich and powerful usually escape censure. As a result, public law often becomes a battleground between advocates of the activist state and those who favour small, passive government.

One would never detect the essentially political character of this conflict by reading the decisions of reviewing courts, the academic literature of the day, or the 1968 *Report of the Royal Commission Inquiry into Civil Rights* (the McRuer Report)[2] – an exhaustive inquiry into administrative decision-making and judicial review in Ontario on which that same senior colleague served as assistant commissioner. Those decisions, that literature, and that report used the conceptual vocabulary of law, not of politics. Inevitably, then, to place this disagreement in its proper context, I have to provide a brief history of traditional administrative law discourse.

Before Canada adopted its *Charter of Rights and Freedoms*, which empowers judges to overturn legislation, even the staunchest proponents of traditional rule-of-law analysis accepted the notion of parliamentary supremacy: the theory that legislatures are entitled to enact laws on virtually any subject, and to define the norms, institutions, and procedures for dealing with that subject, so long as they do so in clear and unequivocal language. Reviewing courts, they acknowledged, could not second-guess the legislature, and therefore could not deal with the desirability, effectiveness, or fairness of legislation.

In a federal state such as Canada, all legislative power was assigned by the constitution to either the provincial or the federal legislature; so long as the legislature in question confined its lawmaking to the subject matter assigned to it, courts could not express any view on the rightness or wrongness of either the policies they adopted or the means chosen to implement those policies. Their function was limited to decoding the intention of the legislature and giving it legal effect.

However, as any sensible person will admit, legislators are often somewhat vague about their intentions. If nothing else, they have to deal with contentious matters in the context of rapidly evolving social or economic circumstances, often with little past experience to guide them. In such circumstances, legislatures tend to use vague, open-ended language to endow administrative agencies with broad mandates to diagnose and remedy the problem at hand. This very vagueness is what allows reviewing judges so much latitude in interpreting legislation, a latitude they frequently use to produce the social outcome that seems right to them. Unfortunately, this outcome may differ from the one contemplated by the legislature, embraced by agencies charged with administering the statute, or endorsed by experts in the field.

Judges, of course, do not wish to be seen to be substituting their view of policy for that of democratically elected legislators. Consequently, they have developed a vocabulary of justification that makes their position seem legitimate, even inevitable. They ostensibly seek to establish whether the government agency administering the statute has acted "without jurisdiction" – outside the scope of authority parliament intended to give it – or has even "lost jurisdiction," by "asking itself the wrong question." In either case, the judges reason, "surely" no sensible person would allow the agency's action to stand.

In addition, courts have adopted a series of procedural presumptions that, supposedly, protect citizens without directly challenging the right of legislatures to override these presumptions if they choose to do so. Thus it is presumed that statutes will "surely" not be applied retroactively or extraterritorially, in the absence of a clear contrary signal from the legislature. Legislatures are also presumed to intend that administrative agencies discharge their regulatory functions "fairly" and, when adjudicating, that they automatically accord citizens "the right to be heard," and other procedural safeguards demanded by the presumption of "natural justice" or "due process."

Not by coincidence, these jurisdictional concerns and procedural presumptions are difficult, if not impossible, to overcome, with the result that judicial review sometimes forces administrative agencies to adopt procedures that impair the effective discharge of their mission, and to adhere to interpretations of their governing statute that produce perverse policy outcomes. Even when legislators attempt to protect administrative agencies from judicial interference by enacting "privative clauses" that forbid courts to review their decisions, judges disingenuously interpret these clauses to mean that the legislature intends to foreclose review only if the agency has acted fairly and within its jurisdiction, but not otherwise.

It would be an understatement to characterize the formal discourse of judicial review as conceptually incoherent and terminologically tortured.[3] However, it would be untrue and unkind to infer that judges intervene in the administration solely to achieve the political outcomes they prefer, rather than those favoured by the legislature and its administrative agents. No less important than judges' political and social values are their professional formation and the institutional limitations of the review process itself. To be a lawyer, one must believe to some extent in law's power and in the benign impact of the legal system; to be a judge, one must be a true believer. Lawyers – and especially judges – thus tend to accept that legal analysis produces optimal social outcomes and (as I suggest in chapter 5) to view other forms of analysis, other bodies of expert knowledge, with suspicion or condescension. However, regulatory agencies are generally designed and staffed on the basis of quite different assumptions: that the physical and social sciences provide much better insights than law into many regulatory issues; that the fact-finding methods employed by those disciplines should be used in preference to those traditionally used by courts; and that while lawyers should not be excluded from regulatory proceedings, neither should they be allowed to dominate them or to derail their outcomes by way of subsequent judicial review proceedings. Finally, it is hardly counter-intuitive to note that judicial review is most often sought by corporate litigants that can afford to litigate, not by the intended beneficiaries of regulation, who usually cannot.

Despite all these shortcomings, challenges to administrative action and state regulation succeed fairly frequently, overturning well-informed decisions of tribunals, agencies, and ministries that would have benefitted not only individual litigants but often the broader public interest as well. Worse yet, even when review proceedings do not succeed, corporate litigants with deep pockets are often able to use them to delay the coming into effect of regulatory decisions and to continue their undesirable or illegal practices in the interim. Worst of all, over the long term, the threat of judicial review clearly deters some government agencies from taking an expansive view of their mandate to protect the public interest.

But it isn't just the practical and political consequences of judicial review that have troubled me throughout my career; it is what reading administrative law judgments taught me about the judicial process. Especially in the 1960s and 1970s (things are somewhat better today), the decisions of reviewing courts were so badly reasoned and written that one could only conclude that reviewing judges first decided how they wanted each case to turn out and then selected a form of words that made such a result appear not only legally inevitable but politically admirable.[4] I acknowledge that my aversion to judicial review is not widely shared. Other scholars will point out, not unfairly, that my views may be influenced by my own unhappy experiences with the process. Two of my own arbitration decisions were overturned on dubious grounds, and with deleterious consequences both for the parties' relationship and for the process of arbitration itself.[5] Over time, I concluded that neither personal irk with the judges, nor professional dismay at the concepts they deployed and the outcomes they produced, constituted a sound basis for academic critique, so I decided to ask some fundamental questions about judicial review. Where had it come from and when? What was its constitutional underpinning? By what legal or political logic could it be justified? How might administrative errors or abuses be prevented or cured in some other way, if not by reviewing courts?

As things stood prior to the adoption of the Charter, the answers to these questions were not obvious. Canada's 1867 constitution made no explicit reference to judicial review. However, given that we have "a constitution similar in principle to that of the United Kingdom," our courts must have inherited their reviewing authority from British courts. But what power did British courts have? These questions led me to me to launch my most ambitious academic project yet, a history of the nineteenth-century English administrative state, entitled "Without the Law."[6] Traditional scholarship held that the superior courts of England had "inherent power" to review the administration – a power they needed in order to discharge their responsibilities as ultimate custodians of "the rule of law" and to ensure (as one court put it) that "there must be no Alsatia where the King's Writ does not run."[7] This was, at best, a bootstraps argument, even a tautology: "we have the power to review because that's what we do." However, contrary to the traditional narrative, the evidence suggests that if judges always had "inherent" power to review the administration, they used it very sparingly until well on in the nineteenth century; and far from being indispensable for "the rule of law," judicial review when it was invoked seemed often to allow private power and privilege to trump the interests of ordinary people. More to the point, as my historical research revealed, the superior courts enjoyed neither a monopoly of adjudication nor a clear mandate to force other decision-making bodies to comply with "the law" as judges understood it.

As to this latter point, common law and parliamentary legislation never did comprise the totality of "law" that "ruled" in England. Three other systems were at least as important as the formal system of law dispensed by the superior courts. Criminal cases were largely decided by lay magistrates who were supposed to apply state criminal law but in practical terms exercised wide discretion which they often used (and abused) to protect the interests of local oligarchs or to advance local versions of social morality. The vast majority of ordinary civil cases was decided by the lay judges of "courts of request" whose mandate was to decide according to "equity and good conscience," or by courts set up to administer medieval systems of customary law or to adjudicate the traditional rights of specific communities. And finally, commercial disputes were most frequently decided according to "the custom of the trade" by arbitrators or by members of domestic tribunals associated with particular sectors of the economy. In sum, the superior courts, and the legal system they administered, made at most a marginal contribution to the "rule of law" in mid-Victorian England. By contrast, the law that actually "ruled" was highly pluralistic – a plethora of legal regimes administered by bodies with different mandates, applying different systems of substantive "law," and deploying different evidentiary and procedural rules.

This led me to ask: if the superior courts did not possess a monopoly over adjudication, if other legal systems had always governed large swathes of English social and economic life and still did so throughout the nineteenth century, how could the superior courts claim the "inherent" right to review those "other" systems to ensure that they conformed to the so-called "ordinary" law of the land of which judges were the ostensible custodians? To answer that question, I had to dig deep into the origins of the administrative state, which appeared early in the nineteenth century as a political and legal response to the social and economic dislocation caused by the industrial revolution. Its very appearance (I argued) was a repudiation of the common and statute law system that supposedly "ruled," but had utterly failed to deal with that dislocation. It was because of that failure, I argued, that administrative law was assigned to a new system of tribunals and inspectorates whose normative and procedural arrangements differed dramatically from those of the superior courts. Nor did the superior courts often seek to ensure compliance with "the rule of law" by reviewing the new administrative regimes, though other strategies were used to attack them.

In short, *"Without the Law"* made a persuasive case that the superior courts in Victorian England enjoyed neither a monopoly over adjudication nor, as a practical matter, effective control over other legal systems. So far as I know, no recent scholarship has challenged my description of England's pluralistic legal system, so this new historical perspective might well have led people to revise or abandon traditional justifications of judicial review. However – unfortunately from my point of view – just as my study was nearing completion in the early 1980s, four near-simultaneous developments made my stand against judicial review pretty much untenable.

The first was the Canadian Supreme Court's belated discovery that our constitution did, after all, entrench the right of citizens to challenge administrative action through judicial review proceedings.[8] The fact that this judgment was written by Chief Justice Laskin, who in his previous professorial incarnation had taken the opposite view, pained me personally but did not diminish its legal force and intellectual respectability. Second, the constitution itself was dramatically amended by the adoption of the Charter, which overturned previous notions of parliamentary supremacy and installed the courts as final arbiters of most legal and political issues. Third, the Supreme Court began to accord much greater deference to administrative decisions and to exercise much greater self-restraint in the exercise of its reviewing powers.[9] This did not cure the doctrinal incoherence of its decisions, but at least the practical consequences of those decisions were less harmful that they had previously been. And finally, the political context of judicial review changed considerably. In the first two or three decades of my career as an administrative lawyer, judicial review had had the effect of destabilizing administrative regimes designed to protect citizens from abuses of private power. However, starting in the 1980s, governments increasingly favoured neo-liberal policies such as balanced budgets, retrenchment of the welfare state, deregulation of markets, and adoption of more draconian regimes of social control. In this new environment, judicial review might potentially be used to slow down the shift to neo-liberalism, and to mitigate the severity of these new regimes.[10]

All of these changes rendered pretty much irrelevant my long-standing preoccupation with the tangled historical roots and dysfunctional contemporary practice of judicial review. Given the enhanced role of judges in Canada's new constitutional regime, judicial review was clearly here to stay; given the new-found willingness of judges to accept administrative interpretations of regulatory legislation, my pragmatic arguments against judicial review lost much of their force; and given the shift in judges' emphasis from protecting the economic freedom of businesses to protecting ordinary citizens from abuse at the hands of public officials, it was increasingly difficult for me to crank up the moral indignation that had fueled my scholarship in this field up to the 1980s. It became clear that I had to take my administrative law scholarship in a new direction because fundamental changes in our political economy had created a crisis in public administration.

In my post-presidential scholarship, I have frequently argued that "globalization of the mind" has generated a broad policy consensus amongst "right-thinking people" around the world – academics, civil servants, editorial writers, business executives, and politicians – that markets produce better social outcomes than regulatory interventions by the state.[11] This consensus was particularly important in Canada, which was "trapped in North America"[12] – tightly bound to the United States not just by NAFTA and other trade regimes but by close and long-standing cultural, educational, social, professional, and investment ties. In recent years, my research showed, "Corporate Canada" had been "hollowed out."[13] Local subsidiaries of transnational corporations had been brought more directly under the close control of US parent firms; their product mandates had been narrowed, their right to make crucial decisions about investments, employment, advertising, and research and development had been diminished; and in some cases, they had been turned into mere corporate shells or closed down altogether. As a result, the interests of Canadian workers, consumers, and communities were increasingly likely to be disregarded by corporate decision-makers located in other countries and preoccupied with global strategies.[14]

How would this new political economy affect public law? I was pessimistic. Canadian governments of all stripes were abandoning the policies and institutions that had expressed the ideals and delivered (albeit imperfectly) on the commitments of the interventionist state. They were, in effect, making globalization and neo-liberalism irreversible by binding successor governments through new trade treaties, new institutional arrangements, new quasi-constitutional practices, new rhetorics and policy logics which would make it impossible for subsequent governments to protect citizens against the abuses of private power – abuses likely to become more frequent in light of the scope accorded to unfettered markets and the freedom given to corporate actors.[15] We were moving towards a "new normal" of lowered public expectations and, ultimately, a "new normal" of less progressive administrative attitudes and programs.[16]

Old habits die hard, I acknowledge. The "new economy" scenario revived my old concerns about judicial review. Since proponents of neo-liberalism often identified the judiciary as "the least dangerous branch" of government,[17] its role in the new political economy would likely be enhanced. Not only would the judiciary help to disempower the executive and legislative arms of government, thereby weakening the regulatory capacities of the state; its new-found role at the centre of the polity, ostensibly to protect "the rule of law," would endow neo-liberalism with an air of respectability that, in my view, it did not deserve.

Clearly, I was edging back towards a more serious involvement with constitutional law, the subject that I had never been allowed to teach. Fortunately, I had managed to maintain a toehold in the field over the intervening years.

My first professional brush with constitutional law occurred in 1961, when I was retained by the Canadian Jewish Congress (CJC) to explore the possibility of a legal challenge to the program of Protestant religious instruction that, beginning in 1943, committed Ontario's previously secular public schools to ensuring that students accept "the historic Christian faith." Presumably the intent of the program was to align Ontario symbolically with the then-beleaguered

United Kingdom which had (and still has) an official state religion. However, it had a direct impact on me as a grade five student: it triggered several unpleasant schoolyard confrontations with anti-semitic classmates. In the course of my research, I was introduced to some of the more obscure elements of Canada's constitution. A seldom-cited pre-confederation statute – the Freedom of Worship Act – still in force in Ontario; the unwritten "provincial constitution" mentioned in the Constitution Act but almost never invoked; implicit guarantees of civil liberties (this was long before the *Charter of Rights and Freedoms*: none of these, I concluded, was likely to convince a court to strike down Ontario's program of religious studies. (I did detect a technical flaw in the regulations governing the program that offered better prospects.)

In the end, the program was abandoned because it was unsustainable in light of the increasing diversity of Ontario's communities and schools. The lesson that political and social pressure can often accomplish what litigation cannot has remained one of my many "unsound" views on the constitution. However, my relationship with the CJC soon ended. I was asked to write another opinion supporting the constitutional right of the Jewish community to have its own tax-supported parochial schools. This, I felt, was not only bad law; it was bad public policy and bad for the community as well. Likewise, legislation outlawing hate propaganda, which I not only declined to support but actively and publicly opposed as an infringement on freedom of expression.[18]

My original research on religious education did produce one dramatic outcome. Reading through nineteenth-century court decisions on education, I discovered that Ontario had experienced a concerted effort by local inhabitants to exclude black students from the public schools – a campaign that looked very like that being conducted in the 1960s by racist US communities against the desegregation of schools mandated by *Brown v Board of Education*. And then I discovered, to my horror, that as of 1962 Ontario still had on its statute books something called *The Coloured Separate Schools Act*, which authorized the creation of a segregated school system for black students. I revealed my discoveries in an article in a legal journal;[19] they were publicized by a journalist; and virtually the same day, Ontario's then-minister of Education, Bill Davis, rose in the legislature to announce that the *Coloured Separate Schools Act* would be repealed forthwith.

At about the same time, in the early to mid-1960s, I was invited to help resuscitate the Canadian Civil Liberties Association (CCLA), which had made its brief debut at the end of the war to protest the mistreatment of Japanese Canadians and then was laid to rest in the filing cabinet of Irving Himel, a Toronto lawyer. I was elected early on as a vice-president and ultimately, in 1976, as president. After a number of false starts, and after being reprieved from bankruptcy by a timely but anonymous gift of $100,000, we were finally able to stabilize the organization under the leadership of Alan Borovoy, an old university friend, whom I recruited from a labour-affiliated human rights organization at the end of the 1960s. Borovoy led the CCLA – he *was* the CCLA – for the next forty years, a term of office that produced many brilliant successes but lasted rather longer than might have been healthy for the organization.

Himel's initiative to revive the CCLA was a response to the proposed establishment of a so-called provincial "crime commission" with extraordinary powers of investigation. A public hue and cry resulted not only in the abandonment of the original proposal but in the creation of the McRuer Commission which, as I have mentioned, turned out to be a landmark (if conceptually arid) inquiry into administrative law. Far more important for Canadian democracy was Prime Minister Trudeau's invocation of the War Measures Act in response to the FLQ crisis of October 1970. The CCLA vigorously and rightly, but unsuccessfully, opposed the federal government's tough action.

My memory of the period is dominated by two events. In the first, then-justice minister John Turner sent a car to collect Borovoy and me from an anti-War Measures rally in Ottawa and took us off to a secret two-day discussion with his officials and other experts on how to replace the Act with more sensible legislation. Then, late on the evening before the 1970 Grey Cup game, I was one of a dozen or so vocal opponents of the act invited to meet privately with the prime minister for an off-the-record, no-holds-barred discussion of the October events. If Trudeau's invocation of the War Measures Act struck me as a repudiation of his supposedly liberal values, his willingness to engage in vigorous debate with a room full of "nobodies" impressed me as a guarantee that at some level, he was still the man in whom we had placed so much hope just a few years earlier.

That guarantee was meant to be redeemed by Trudeau's introduction, ten years later, of the Canadian *Charter of Rights and*

Freedoms. Unfortunately, the Charter caused a deep split within the CCLA executive. Some members viewed a constitutionally entrenched charter as a fundamental and irreversible national commitment to the values of democracy, human rights, and social justice. Others, myself included, were more skeptical. Enhancing the power of the judiciary, we feared, could lead to the striking down of progressive legislation, as it had done during the era of the US New Deal and likely would in Canada, given the generally conservative record of our courts in labour, human rights, and other contexts. Fortunately (from my point of view) the ultimate draft of the Charter contained the "notwithstanding" clause, which offers legislatures a time-limited power to override its provisions. This seemed like a reasonable compromise both to most people in the CCLA and to key political actors across the country.

I played occasional walk-on parts during the decade of constitutional negotiations that followed repatriation of the constitution and the entrenchment of the Charter. For example, I was part of a small group that advised Ontario's then-premier, Bob Rae, during the negotiations leading up to the Charlottetown Accord (the Accord was decisively rejected in a national referendum). I predicted that the Supreme Court's historic antipathy to labour would leave workers and unions without recourse under the Charter (I was proved wrong)[20] and advised union lawyers not to entrust their clients' futures to the Supreme Court (the jury is still out).[21] In later years, I made the case for the federal government to take a lead role in labour market and industrial relations policy (a good argument that was ignored by governments at every level, and rejected by the Supreme Court as well).[22] And I predicted that right-wing populism was leading to constitutional changes that would entrench neoliberalism as a fundamental principle of our polity (not that the effort wasn't made – but it failed).[23] All in all, none of my forays into constitutional law did much to call into question the judgment of my senior colleague at the beginning of my career.

On the other hand, I was not the only would-be constitutionalist whose interventions consistently missed the mark. More specifically, both those who favoured and those who feared the Charter turned out to be wrong. Canada's Supreme Court has seldom used the Charter to strike down market regulation, though it has occasionally interpreted the Charter's procedural protections to make the job of regulation more difficult for interventionist governments. Nor has the

Court failed to use the Charter in favour of disadvantaged groups. On the contrary, its rulings have generally expanded protection for such groups and enhanced respect for human rights and democratic practices. The problem is that Supreme Court rulings do not in themselves change anything except the law and, as it turns out, the law does not change the deep structures of the economy, culture, society, or polity. With a co-author I asked the awkward question, "Does the Charter Matter?"[24] "Not much," we concluded, after reviewing social data that described the actual impact of twenty years of litigation. Groups that were the intended beneficiaries of the Charter still suffered considerable discrimination and disadvantage; police practices and penal policies had, if anything, become more harsh rather than less so; abusive behaviour by public officials in their dealings with immigrants, the poor, and other vulnerable persons did not seem to have abated; the quality of our parliamentary democracy remained unchanged at best, and had in some respects deteriorated.

Ten years later, I did another study of the impact of Charter decisions on labour and employment law, my field of special expertise. The Supreme Court, contrary to my earlier predictions, has shown remarkable sympathy for unions and workers. Nonetheless, during the period when workers and unions were winning most of their court battles (in both Charter and non-Charter cases) labour was losing members, influence, power, and share of GDP.[25]

In a series of articles, I sought to explain why constitutional litigation so often fails to achieve its objectives and why the courts cannot perform the heavy lifting of social or economic transformation. The "real constitution," I maintained – the constitution that determines the actual relationship between citizens and governments and amongst the branches of government – is inscribed not in the document that bears that name but rather in the deep structures of political economy.[26] Epidemiologists have shown that as one descends a social and economic gradient from the richest citizens to the poorest, one encounters diminished life-expectancy and an increased incidence of poor health. I argued that educational and job opportunities, participation in political and cultural activities, respectful treatment from public and corporate officials, and enjoyment of human rights and civil liberties are also unevenly distributed along that same gradient.[27] Worse yet, demography changes along the gradient: the closer you get to the bottom, the more you are likely to encounter racialized minorities and women, recent immigrants and aboriginal peoples, people with disabilities, and young, poorly educated people. In short, the real constitution does not deliver on the promises of the formal constitution; rather it retards their fulfilment by concealing its failures.

Social change, I argue now as I did at the beginning of my career, requires changes in the distribution of wealth and power. Only the state can effect such a redistribution and the state will act only when economically subordinate groups mobilize to win political power or to influence its exercise. Coincidentally, in 1961, the year I began teaching, Pierre Trudeau (then a legal academic) urged in a law review article that "every social order should guarantee the rights of man, as a consumer and as a producer."[28] His views weren't very different from the ones that led to my being banned from teaching constitutional law, but they do not seem to have blighted his career to quite the same extent as they did mine. After all, he did manage to persuade a somewhat dubious country to adopt *The Canadian Charter of Rights and Freedoms* a scant twenty years later. It is worth noting, though, that Trudeau's 1982 Charter makes little mention of economic rights, and none at all of the rights of "producers" or "consumers."

Irony is my favourite indoor sport, so I will conclude this chapter on an ironic note. The senior colleague whose intervention prevented me from teaching constitutional law was not only a highly regarded constitutional lawyer but also a formidable legislative draftsman. After his death, an annual award was established in his honour by Ontario's attorney general as "a kind of Pulitzer Prize for legal writing." In 1987, I became the second recipient of that award.

Legal Education and the Legal Profession – So Near and Yet So Far

I never intended to be a legal academic, much less to make legal education one of my main scholarly interests, and I certainly never imagined that my choice of career would place me at arm's length from the legal profession itself, which I had hoped to enter for as long as can remember.

I have explained elsewhere how I came to join the Osgoode faculty in 1961; now a word about why I chose to remain there for the next forty-four years. At the very outset of my career, I turned down offers from young law faculties in Singapore and Dar-es-Salaam. A few years later, in 1965 (as recounted in chapter 1), I declined offers from two well-established Canadian faculties, McGill and the University of Toronto. But the truth is that it was not Osgoode's virtues that kept me there through the early to mid-1960s but its shortcomings, and the challenge of overcoming them.

In pretty much every respect, Osgoode at the beginning of the 1960s was not what it ought to have been. The curriculum was uninspiring. First-year courses had remained unchanged for decades and students were offered few opportunities to select optional subjects in the upper years. Teaching mainly consisted of formal lectures delivered to large classes, often by practising lawyers who served as part-time instructors. Some senior members of both the full-time and the part-time faculty lectured in their barrister's gowns – the symbolic incarnation of legal orthodoxy. Most senior professors were not prolific scholars and those who were (with perhaps one exception) produced traditional doctrinal scholarship. Although Osgoode attracted some fine students thanks to its historic monopoly of legal education in Ontario, virtually any applicant who met minimum standards was admitted. This did not make for an exciting intellectual atmosphere. Moreover, some students just wanted to be taught "The Law" in a straightforward manner and were indifferent – even hostile – to attempts at curricular or pedagogic innovation.

Osgoode's administration was academically conservative and somewhat heavy-handed. As my own experience of being denied the chance to teach constitutional law suggests, academic freedom was by no means assured. Or to cite another example: a member of the faculty with considerable scholarly promise but a critical demeanor was denied tenure by the dean, who responded to my protest by noting that the person in question was "too short" to dominate the large classes that we were obliged to teach. Even the physical facilities were unsatisfactory. Although the law school occupied a handsome 1930s addition to a beautiful Georgian building (home to the profession's governing body and the province's superior and appellate courts), our classrooms and library were badly designed, there were too few offices to accommodate faculty growth, and students had virtually no space to call their own.

I should not overstate the inadequacies of the school. A couple of the senior professors were dynamic teachers and/or productive scholars. Almost all of them were kind to and popular with their students and affable enough with their younger colleagues (though two made casual anti-semitic remarks to me). And the dean, to be fair, was determined to enhance Osgoode's academic ethos and reputation, as evidenced by his hiring of six or eight young, progressive, and research-minded recruits, myself included.

This latter fact gave me hope. Within a year or two of my joining Osgoode, it was becoming clear that we had entered an era of significant change. Though we all knew the decade was the 1960s, we gradually became aware that we were living through "the sixties" – a time of turbulence for professions, academic institutions, intellectual traditions, social relations, and lifestyles. At Osgoode as elsewhere, this turbulence was driven in large measure by demography. In 1962 our governing body, the Law Society, belatedly acknowledged that the law school would have to grow considerably in order to accommodate the looming cohort of baby-boomers that would soon be seeking admission to the bar. Growth obviously required an expansion of our faculty complement, and as our numbers increased, the balance of opinion within the faculty began to favour a more up-to-date model of North American legal education. This shift, however, was difficult to achieve, given our physical arrangements, embedded traditions, and governance structures.

Our location in the historic "Osgoode Hall" complex made it hard for faculty and students to get out from under the long shadow of the profession and the courts.

To cite one notorious example, in the spring of 1966, faculty members received a decanal memorandum complaining that a student had been sighted within the precincts of the law school dressed in a checked shirt, jeans, and army boots, rather than a jacket and tie. All members of faculty were enjoined to ensure that students maintain standards of dress appropriate to our professional setting and mission. This was merely the symbolic representation of a substantive problem. So long as we were located in close proximity to the nation's densest concentration of legal practitioners, so long as those practitioners remained a dominant influence in our teaching program, so long as students were tacitly encouraged to align themselves with the legal culture around them rather than take a critical distance from it, so long as the law school remained isolated from the leavening intellectual and social influence of other academic faculties, change would be difficult to achieve.

Nor did the school's landlord and governing body, the Law Society, seem likely to permit significant change, much less to encourage it. A few years earlier, in 1957, the Law Society had only grudgingly recognized degrees awarded by several Ontario universities as the equivalent of those awarded by Osgoode, its own proprietary law school. However, some members of the governing body remained suspicious of the legal academy, as law professors began to experiment more extensively with new teaching techniques and to write critically about legal rules and institutions and the profession itself. In the spirit of the times, the junior faculty became increasingly disenchanted with both the dean's relatively conservative views on legal education and his administrative style. This portended difficulties for their relations with the governing body which, for its part, wanted above all not to re-open the controversy it thought it had laid to rest in 1957. And finally, though growth and change would be expensive, the Law Society received no government funding to support the law school's operations.

On 17 March 1965, a proverbial "dark and stormy night," matters came to a head. At an unprecedented dinner meeting convened on short notice by the Law Society, the faculty was told that York

University had offered to adopt Osgoode Hall Law School as its own faculty of law, that the school would move physically to York's new suburban campus, and that the Law Society had decided to accept the offer subject to negotiation of suitable terms. I was the first faculty member to react. "A wonderful idea!" I said. "Count on me." My dean expressed rather less enthusiasm. "If there were a dozen things to do with the law school," he said, "moving to York would be number thirteen on my list."

Then ensued many months of rancorous debate, secret plotting, and increasingly bizarre counter-proposals by the dean and others opposed to the move.[1] By early 1966, however, negotiations with York University had been successfully concluded, the dean had resigned, and several senior professors had announced their departure as well. Meanwhile, the junior faculty had been augmented by several excellent recruits and in July 1967, following an interim deanship, invigorated by the arrival of a new dean, the charismatic Gerald Le Dain.[2] This shift in the leadership, demographics, and outlook of the faculty afforded its insurgent members – "Radio Free Osgoode" we jokingly called ourselves – the opportunity to take practical control of the new law faculty at York.

And what an opportunity it was. Here we were, in effective charge of Canada's largest, second-oldest, and (so we thought) most conservative law school, with a mandate to re-invent it, ample funds to do so from an education-friendly provincial government, the blessings of the profession's governing body, the enthusiastic support of an ambitious new university, at a unique historical moment when progressive change was taking place all around us. That is why I stayed at Osgoode and how I came to find myself at the centre of a major project of institution building, initially as self-designated "planning coordinator" and, from January 1968, as associate dean.

We quickly established a building committee chaired by Dennis Hefferon, an expert in urban planning law. Over the next few years academic policy reviews, chaired by future deans Stanley Beck and Peter Hogg, opened up the curriculum to new perspectives; faculty scholarship took a serious turn to interdisciplinarity and we hired Hans Mohr, one of the first social scientists to be appointed to the full-time faculty of a Canadian law school; new teaching methods were introduced, culminating in the establishment of Parkdale Community Legal Services, a poverty law centre and teaching clinic led by Fred Zemans; the graduate program was expanded (I directed it and taught a graduate seminar in legal education); and a certificate program was introduced for non-lawyers who wanted to study law.

As applications to Osgoode increased exponentially, we ratcheted up admission standards, but also introduced a new equity stream to ensure that outstanding candidates who lacked conventional credentials were not excluded. These early years following the move to York also saw a rapid increase in the enrolment of women and, less rapidly, but as quickly as we could manage it, in the appointment of women to the faculty. Finally, the formal governance and informal culture of the law school changed dramatically, as we grew comfortable in our new home, no longer dominated by the ethos of the courts and the profession. Students were invited to join the faculty council; they developed an array of extra-curricular organizations and a calendar of social events; and their sartorial preferences strayed increasingly from professional standards without decanal regret or reproach. By the time I became dean, in 1972, Osgoode had gained a reputation as Canada's most innovative law school, and I had learned a great deal about legal scholarship and pedagogy.

I had also learned a thing or two about the legal profession. By happenstance, a year or two before the affiliation with York came to dominate our agenda, I had made contact with Robert Mathews, a distinguished American labour law scholar with an interest in legal ethics. Mathews had the idea of seeding ethical problems throughout the labour law casebook that he edited so that students would encounter them naturally, in the context of thinking about substantive problems, rather than in a special course on legal ethics, where they would appear in more abstract form. He wanted some information on Canadian legal ethics, especially as they might affect the practice of labour law. In trying to answer his queries, I discovered that virtually nothing had been written on legal ethics in this country; that unlike those in the United States, disciplinary proceedings in Ontario (and I believe other provinces) did not culminate in reasoned decisions; and that, as a consequence, no body of case law had developed to provide guidance to practitioners or regulators. I also found that not a single Canadian academic was teaching or writing about the legal profession. In 1965, I set out to remedy that egregious omission by offering the first course ever taught on the subject in this country.

In order to do so, I had to educate myself about the profession. For example, I needed to know where and how lawyers practised. No one could provide such information. The Canadian Bar Association (CBA) had undertaken a survey of the profession in the late 1940s, but its findings were never published in full. Nor had they been updated in subsequent decades. Statistics Canada advised me they did not collect data about lawyers or other "special interest groups" (though I had been surveyed by that very agency a few weeks earlier about the electrical appliances in our household). When I asked the Law Society staff how many lawyers practised in Ontario, they had no ready answer for me but kindly produced one by dividing that year's total bank deposits by the dollar value of the annual fees paid by each lawyer and then including those who were delinquent in paying their fees. In despair, I finally conducted my own study of the Toronto legal profession in 1971,[3] but failed to inspire imitators (or attract readers) in academe, the profession, or the government. Lacking sociological or economic studies as a basis for analysis or critique, throughout the 1970s I had to focus my scholarship on speculative and conceptual issues such as the governance of the profession, its social responsibilities, and, of course, its education.[4]

In the meantime, perhaps by virtue of being Canada's only academic in the field, I had somehow achieved sufficient visibility as an "expert" that in 1969, I was appointed to the Canadian Bar Association's committee to revise its code of professional responsibility. The experience confirmed all my worst fears about the profession. The CBA Code had been promulgated in 1920. However, as the CBA had no regulatory authority, its code could serve as the basis of professional discipline only if it was adopted by the provincial law societies. This had not happened. Indeed, the Code had virtually disappeared from view: in the fifty years since its publication, it had apparently never been cited in any legal publication, nor, during that time, despite dramatic changes in Canadian society, was the code ever amended. While our committee did its best to inform itself about the practices of the profession's governing bodies and developments in professional regulation in the US and the UK, we proceeded (as most lawyers' committees do) on the basis of anecdotal evidence and intuited conclusions. The new code we produced was certainly an improvement over the 1920 version and, unlike its predecessor, it was formally adopted by law societies in most Canadian provinces. However, it too was embellished with clichés, riddled with contradictions, and willfully oblivious to the political economy of legal practice. Not much can be done in the absence of facts – but lawyers (of all people!) seem to have an "invincible repugnance" to facts, especially to social facts that might ground systemic analysis and policy initiatives.

I continued to lecture and publish on legal education and the legal profession and, at the end of the 1970s, became even more deeply involved with policy development in both fields. In 1979 I was elected a bencher, a member of the Law Society's governing body, with one of the highest votes of any candidate, and in 1980, I was appointed chair of the Social Sciences and Humanities Research Council (SSHRC) of Canada's Consultative Group on Legal Education and Research. In chapter 9 I summarize the latter's findings and recommendations; accordingly, in this chapter I will focus on my brief career as a bencher. Convocation (the plenary body of benchers) comprised forty elected members, four lay members appointed by the government to protect the public interest, and a significant number of honorary and *ex officio* members, few of whom participated actively in its deliberations. However, those deliberations were themselves relatively infrequent, and often inconsequential. Much of the work of Convocation was delegated to committees. Foremost amongst these was the discipline committee on which we all served; its members sat in panels of three to hear complaints against individual lawyers. While the accused lawyer usually received something approximating due process from the hearing panel, the overall disciplinary scheme was marred by the availability of an appeal to Convocation sitting *en banc*. There, members who had not heard the evidence often supplemented the record with exculpatory or condemnatory testimonials based on their personal knowledge of the miscreant or the complainant and/or with general ruminations on community sentiment and public relations.

No issue of public policy or professional governance engaged the attention of Convocation to the same degree as discipline. In part, this was because Convocation lacked both a policy committee and the staff capacity to provide analysis or information on which to base policy decisions. My proposal to remedy both these omissions ultimately received grudging acceptance, and until I completed my four-year term as a bencher, I served as chair of a new "policy and planning" committee. (The committee was abolished when my term ended.) In part, however, Convocation's apparent indifference to policy and the systemic analysis on which policy ought to be based stemmed from what is sometimes called *déformation professionelle*

– the tendency of intense professional training or experience to narrow or skew one's perspectives. Lawyers are trained to deal with individual transactions or controversies; they generally do so well enough in their professional practice but are unused to and/or uncomfortable with systemic analysis. This exposure to the shortcomings of the profession's policy-making process influenced my near-contemporaneous review of legal education and research, and led me to favour the broadening of law school curricula as described in chapter 9. It also shaped my scholarly agenda insofar as my subsequent work on the legal profession tilted very much in the direction of systemic analysis and critique. Happily, Ontario's Law Society has since addressed some of the shortcomings I witnessed: it now conducts significant sociological research to support its extensive diversity initiatives, it has reformed its discipline procedures, and it has launched numerous debates on the larger, long-term issues confronting the profession.

My four years as a member of the profession's governing body also provided me with insights into its political economy. In very general terms, the membership of Convocation in those days comprised three groups: high profile civil or criminal advocates who often practised alone or in boutique firms; members of large, powerful corporate firms; and general practitioners from small firms in suburban communities or county towns. Members of the first group were highly respected as the embodiment of the historic traditions of an independent bar; members of the second were obviously aligned with their corporate clients but nonetheless exhibited a (to me) surprising sensitivity to the Law Society's broad public responsibilities; and members of the third were particularly aggressive in seeking to protect the economic interests of their fellow practitioners and were the least sympathetic to innovations in legal education and reforms in the profession's organization and governance. Not surprisingly, the three groups tended to clash over such issues as the certification of specialists, mandatory continuing education, the limitation of numbers entering the profession, and relations between the profession and the legal academy. (To set the record straight, Convocation now includes a significant phalanx of reform-minded benchers many of whom are women, members of racialized groups, or from non-conventional practice settings.)

I also observed first-hand what (mainly US) sociological studies were beginning to document: that the profession as a whole was fractured both vertically (between specialists and generalists, and amongst specialists) and horizontally (between its elites and lesser orders). These sub-groups not only served different clienteles and reaped different rewards, they possessed different kinds of professional knowledge and inhabited different professional cultures. And finally, they tended to draw their members from different demographic groups. These insights informed much of what I was to write on the subject in later years.

Initially, I worked with a group of scholars interested in the sociology of the legal profession and contributed to an international comparative volume on the subject.[5] Later, my focus broadened and I began to speculate on the effect of changes in Canada's economy and society on the organization, regulation, and delivery of legal education, knowledge, and services. "Would traditional forms of professional self-government survive?" I asked; "Would locally-based law firms be replaced by global firms?" "Would these firms remain recognizable as law firms – or would they morph into interdisciplinary firms encompassing both lawyers and professionals in adjacent disciplines?" "Would much of the routine work of lawyering be performed by computers?" And "what did all of this portend for legal education and scholarship?"[6]

These speculations drew on my contemporaneous work in political economy as well as on the writings of other socio-legal scholars, and seemed to offer a promising way to explain what was happening to the profession. However, I clearly underestimated a development whose impact was in fact entirely predictable: the restructuring of Canada's economy in the 1980s and 1990s was causing major dislocations in the legal profession. Globalization and the ensuing realignment of corporate wealth and power (what I described in chapter 4 as the "hollowing out of corporate Canada")[7] led to the growth of first national and then global law firms, with a commensurate decline in the prospects of locally based firms. Then, starting around 2000, corporate clients decided to reduce their expenditure on legal fees by establishing or enlarging their in-house legal departments and insisting on more client-friendly billing practices by outside counsel. The law firms that served these prime clients embarked on various expansionary and cost-cutting strategies, strategies that ultimately destroyed their business model. At about the same time, small businesses and middle-class individuals increasingly found that they were able to document routine transactions by using online services, and to hire non-lawyer consultants or paralegals to represent them in minor litigation and debt collection and in their quotidian dealings with government agencies. Finally, technology began to enable many routine but remunerative legal tasks – land registry searches, document reviews, library research – to be performed electronically, more cheaply and, to an extent, offshore. These developments have diminished the demand for legal services or, more accurately, the aggregate expenditures for conventional legal services.

Paradoxically, while an increasingly troubled market ought to have sent signals to aspiring lawyers to switch to other careers, the number of applicants for admission to the bar increased considerably. This was only in part the result of a modest expansion in the number and size of Canadian law faculties. Much more important was the influx (reflux?) of Canadian graduates of law programs in the UK, US, and Australia who had gone to study abroad because they were denied admission to Canadian law schools. The coincidence of a shrinking market for lawyers and a growing supply of law graduates has led to a crisis of confidence in both the profession and the legal academy – a crisis whose effects have been exacerbated by news of a much more extreme crisis in the United States.

Many leaders of the bar, some student groups, and a few law school deans have responded to this troubled situation by embracing legal fundamentalism – a belief system with three related tenets. The first is that recent graduates are facing poor employment prospects because they are not properly educated. This deficiency can be remedied (fundamentalists believe) if law schools place renewed emphasis on teaching "the basics." However (a second tenet of the faith), law schools have abandoned their historic mission of producing "practice ready" lawyers because the professoriate has captured them and converted them into launching pads for esoteric research projects and/or subversive ideologies. And a third fundamentalist position: since the profession's governing bodies see themselves as accountable to the public for the quality of legal services and to their members for creating favourable market conditions, they have the right – indeed the duty – to re-assert the control over legal education that they relinquished *de facto* to university law faculties from the 1960s onwards. The fundamentalist agenda is clear: law schools must be made to produce lawyers who are ready to practise in today's market with minimal subsequent investment by the bar in their socialization or training.

These beliefs, I have argued, are wrong in virtually every respect.[8] Young law graduates are generally much better educated today than they were in previous generations; today's difficult market conditions have nothing to do with legal education and everything to do with the restructuring of Canada's economy; there is no such thing as "the basics" of legal knowledge, or at least no evidence or argument that has so far plausibly identified them; legal practice is so varied that lawyers in different lines of work need to know (and can only afford to know) very different things; being "practice ready" on graduation virtually ensures that a lawyer will soon become "practice obsolete"; the profession's unwillingness or inability to think systemically disqualifies it from a controlling role in the design of legal education, as does the statutory mandate of university senates and faculties to design and implement academic curricula.

Nonetheless, regulations have recently been adopted in all common law provinces that require law schools to ensure that their graduates are equipped with knowledge of a long list of legal fields and "core competencies" that the profession deems essential for legal practice. Non-compliant schools will not be "accredited," and their graduates will not be eligible for a call to the bar. Few law deans protested the introduction of these new arrangements at the time of their adoption, presumably because they reckoned that law societies would merely pretend to regulate and they in turn would pretend to comply. However, my experience as a law student in the 1950s and as a young professor in the 1960s, when law societies exercised the powers they later abandoned and have now reclaimed, persuades me that the deans seriously underestimated the risks to which legal education has been exposed.

In the first place, training students in "competencies" is resource-intensive. Law schools will almost certainly have to divert resources from other activities they now pursue, including the generation of knowledge and critique, public service, and graduate studies. Second, treating law schools as battery farms for the hatching of "practice ready" lawyers undermines their fundamental character as centres of learning and agents of change. These latter activities will not only be attacked by the profession and students alike for siphoning off scarce resources; they will be stigmatized as the source of subversive ideas. Third, the list of courses and competencies made mandatory for professional accreditation shows that the law societies are prepared to legislate on the basis of a fundamentalist notion of what constitutes the practice of law today, without regard for the rapid changes that are occurring in the profession. Worse yet, the list was constructed without any empirical evidence of what Canadian lawyers do or what they know, and in utter disregard of what all serious sociological studies of the profession tell us: that there is no common core of legal knowledge, that there are no universally required lawyer competencies, that there is no single legal culture or model of legal practice. The law societies attempted to respond to this last criticism after the new regulations had already been adopted by conducting an after-the-fact "validation" survey of what skills and knowledge junior lawyers actually needed during their first five years of practice. Suffice it to say that this survey was so technically flawed that its findings cannot be taken seriously. Nor would they be by any regulatory body less inclined to fact-based policy-making than Canada's law societies.

This last point bears elaboration. Within a few years of the coming into force of the new regime, it is already clear that the arrangements for the "accreditation" of law schools were poorly conceived and badly administered. To cite some examples:

- Law schools must ensure that all students have been prepared to enter the private practice of law in accordance with the regulations, although some 30–40 per cent of their graduates ultimately pursue other careers.
- Several offshore institutions have been allowed to offer a full Canadian curriculum to Canadian students, many of whose grades were not high enough to qualify them for admission to a Canadian law school but who were sufficiently affluent to be able to afford a legal education abroad. These offshore institutions are not held to the same requirements as accredited Canadian law schools, though their graduates are deemed admissible to the bar.
- Canadian law schools have already begun to game the accreditation process, paring down their curriculums so as to attract students by offering them shortcuts to graduation and bar admission.[9]
- Because the accreditation standards prescribe only a meaningless list of competencies and courses in which students must be instructed, and do not lay down crucial quality standards for accreditation dealing with such matters as academic freedom or faculty-student ratios, law societies have no proper basis on

which to evaluate new law schools that proclaim their intention to staff up with a low-paid, transient, or part-time faculty or to require professors and students to abide by the teachings of a particular religious faith.[10]

In short, because they lack expertise in legal education, law societies are unlikely to understand the long-term, system-wide implications of decisions they take in the course of accrediting new law schools. However, there is reason to be optimistic about legal education. Law societies are likely to come and go, I maintain, and the legal profession itself is likely to dissolve into a *congeries* of sub-, para- or hybrid professions.[11] Nonetheless, law schools can and will survive, so long as they pursue their true calling as knowledge communities.[12] That is why they must resist the bar's recent ill-considered and poorly executed power-grab and reclaim responsibility for their own fate.

I wish conflict between the legal academy and the profession's governing bodies weren't necessary. I wish above all that the profession had the wisdom to understand that knowledge-seeking critique-generating change-making law schools represent its own best chance of adapting to the future rather than succumbing to it.

Time will tell.

Boundary Crossing – Globalization, Transnational Law, and Comparative Law

I didn't invent globalization. However, I might be the person responsible for its emergence as a recognized category of legal scholarship. In late 1998, I decided to test my electronic research skills by finding everything I had written on the subject. However, when I entered "globalization" into the primitive search engines of the time, I came up empty-handed. A helpful Osgoode librarian explained why: the Library of Congress – taxonomer to the English-speaking world – used the term "international economic integration" rather than "globalization" in its classification system. An e-mail exchange with a sheepish official ensued, and within a few days he advised me that the Library of Congress would henceforth use the term "globalization" instead.

This was welcome news, not least because, as I've mentioned, one of my publications was entitled "Globalization of the Mind."[1] Globalization, I contended, was not only a system of international economic relations; it was an intellectual and ideological consensus amongst "right thinking" people around the world that social ordering was best achieved through reliance on markets, not state action. Countries whose policies contravened this consensus were liable to be punished. Currency-dealers, credit-rating agencies, and bond traders would question the soundness of their economic management; investors would take their capital elsewhere, along with the jobs and tax revenues that investment would generate; and potential trading partners would deny imports from non-conforming countries access to their markets.

All of these possibilities created pressures which few governments (certainly not Canada's) could resist, even if they wished to. And globalization of the mind ensured that they would not wish to. To differing degrees, and in somewhat different fashions, the governments of almost all political stripes in almost all advanced countries began to abandon what had been known as the "postwar consensus" – a tacit understanding between left and right, labour and capital, that markets would be allowed to operate freely, subject to reasonable regulation; that wealth would be modestly redistributed through a system of progressive taxation and social transfers; and that workers would have a voice in the governance of both the polity and their workplaces. In place of this previous understanding, a new consensus emerged: the neo-liberal "Washington consensus" that capital, services, intellectual property, and goods would be allowed to move freely across borders; markets would be significantly deregulated and barriers to access would be eliminated; taxation levels and government programs would be capped or reduced; and workers' protections and entitlements would be rolled back to allow greater managerial flexibility. Margaret Thatcher famously insisted, "There is no alternative" to neo-liberalism. Canada, I argued, was experiencing a second, unique, TINA – "trapped in North America" as it became increasingly integrated into the political, cultural, and economic space of the United States.[2]

Globalization, in my view, had begun to function as a sort of constitution: a statement of fundamental beliefs that attested to, and the institutional architecture that implemented, the new consensus.[3] Trade regimes like the World Trade Organization (WTO), the European Union (EU), and the North American Free Trade Agreement (NAFTA) ensured that both local producers and consumers became integrated into transnational market arrangements. Corporations could raise and invest capital wherever they wished, shift technology, know-how, and production to lower-cost jurisdictions, and use global communications networks and value chains to access new markets and achieve economies of scale. (Parenthetically, the same communications technologies that enabled global corporate expansion also helped criminals and terrorists to send information, drugs, arms, people, and dirty money across borders, and facilitated the spread of diseases, popular culture, and – ironically – emancipatory discourse.) As a result, economies and polities ceased to be congruent, and states were left with diminished ability to protect their own social values, tax revenues, jobs, and ecosystems. Or to put it another way, over the course of two or three decades of globalization, the balance of power between corporations and states and between corporations and the public interest had shifted dramatically, and almost always in favour of corporations.

As someone who still entertained the heretical notion that state power can and should curb abuses of private corporate power, I was deeply concerned about these developments. At the same time, I tried to keep an open mind about globalization. There was no inherent reason why it had to take the form of red-in-tooth-and-claw neo-liberalism. Postwar "internationalism," and its cherished offspring, the European Union, proposed a transnational consensus built around if not social democracy, then a kinder, gentler form of capitalism. Moreover, even in its neo-liberal incarnation, the claims of globalization could not be dismissed altogether: the free flow of ideas and talents along with capital and commerce; open societies, however fragile, emerging in the wake of open markets; cheaper goods and services for consumers in the advanced economies; wealth and wellbeing increasing in the developing world; and ultimately perhaps, even more resources for all governments to attend to the needs of their citizens.

In my early engagement with the subject, I tried earnestly to ferret out evidence that global regulatory structures were emerging – would soon emerge, might conceivably emerge – to fill the void left by the decay of national regimes.[4] Alas, the evidence pointed in the opposite direction. No new *lex laboris* was emerging within global corporations to protect the rights of their workers comparable to the *lex mercatoria* fashioned by arbitrators and by legal and consulting firms to govern cross-border business transactions.[5] Corporate codes of conduct seemed to have little impact on the labour practices of their sponsors, and arguably deflected more promising projects of regulation.[6] Attempts to construct a system of transnational labour law – I finally concluded – were comparable in their futility to the biblical challenge of trying to make bricks without straw.[7]

Globalization also interested me for quite a different reason. As I recount in chapter 10, by around 1980 I had begun to investigate a set of ideas that ultimately became known as "legal pluralism." Essentially, I had come to believe that law need not emanate from the state, that it is inherent in all ongoing social relationships, that it can take forms and operate in ways that bear little resemblance to formal state law, and that in specific contexts it can accomplish all that state law accomplishes, and sometimes more. Globalization represented a perfect opportunity to explore these notions.[8] How would transnational corporations be governed? How would disputes between transnational businesses be resolved? How would transnational regimes of environmental, securities, or labour market regulation develop to ensure that global trade did not generate harms for investors, workers, or communities? And if no such regulatory regimes appeared, would actors within capital markets, workplaces, or ecosystems somehow find a way to safeguard their own interests and resolve their differences?

Some answers were provided by what was coming to be called "transnational law": a somewhat ill-defined body of rules generated by different means and administered by different bodies. Thus, the United Nations (UN) established special tribunals for the former Yugoslavia and Rwanda – and ultimately, a permanent International Criminal Court (ICC) – to try the perpetrators of genocide, crimes against humanity, and war crimes. The International Standards Organization (ISO) promoted the adoption by states, manufacturers, and service providers of uniform product standards to protect consumers. The World Health Organization (WHO), the International Bank for Settlements (IBS), the International Labour Organization (ILO), and countless other organizations of states or networks of state agencies have created a "web of rule" in the areas of economic and social activity specific to their mandates. These all represent potentially useful contributions to "transnational law."

However, the reach of transnational law has so far exceeded its grasp. Our domestic legal systems depend for their legitimacy, in the end, on democratic political systems which have no international counterpart. And they depend for their effectiveness on the executive departments and agencies of government that promote compliance, detect illicit conduct, and enforce sanctions to suppress it – functions not yet widely replicated in the emerging system of transnational law.

Optimists point to what they perceive to be promising new developments in transnational governance. They cite the way in which epistemic communities – communities of experts – transmit ideas from one country to another. Dialogue amongst jurists, they claim, has fostered a process of "judicial globalization" which, in turn, has sensitized courts around the world to human rights issues and provided them with new conceptual tools to better defend them. The advent of social media has empowered "defiant publics" by subjecting repressive regimes to real-time scrutiny and censure from abroad. Social movements, labour unions, and environmental groups have learned to cooperate across national boundaries, they argue, in order to organize successful campaigns, demonstrations, and boycotts against corporations that abuse the environment or their workers. And, optimists contend, although no comprehensive transnational government is in prospect, informal legislative, executive, and adjudicative institutions are emerging that to some extent mimic or replicate state functions. New transnational rule-making bodies adopt codes of conduct or best practice, they insist; new monitoring and reporting bodies promote compliance and detect violations; new compliance strategies are being deployed to punish offenders and deter future misbehaviour.

I wish I could share in this optimism, but most of the hard evidence points in the opposite direction. Despite the best efforts of inspired judges, social justice, human rights, and civil liberties seem to be increasingly endangered, even in the advanced democracies, several of which are now avowedly or functionally "illiberal." The social media, the supposed nervous system of insurgent social movements, have facilitated government snooping and enabled the rise of xenophobic and plutocratic regimes. Societies ostensibly transformed by the "colour revolutions" and "Arab springs" of a few years ago have become authoritarian, corrupt, chaotic, and worse. Important transnational institutions – the EU and NAFTA especially – seem at risk of destabilization or demise. The foreigner, the "other," is demonized and scapegoated in a growing number of both developed and developing countries. And somehow, it is the ideas of the rich, powerful, and nasty – not emancipatory ideas – that seem to travel fastest and farthest, often in apparent disregard of formal legal constraints and the supposedly impermeable barriers of state sovereignty and cultural exceptionalism.[9]

However much I admire the intellectual formulation and normative aspirations of transnational law, these regressive developments make me doubt its power and therefore its promises and prospects. Struggle, I maintain, is what will make the world a better place, not law.[10] But while I am skeptical about the transformative potential of law – whether national or transnational – by no means do I suggest that we ought to ignore its myriad forms and functions. On the contrary, as a matter of simple sociological fact, we use law – law of every type and provenance – to express our values, frame our institutions, organize our relationships, and resolve our disputes. Consequently, I believe that in order to better understand how societies work, we must carefully scrutinize law's sources and strategies, its quotidian operations and long-term effects, its language and culture, its architects and adversaries. This conviction led me to develop an early (albeit intermittent) interest in comparative labour law.

In chapter 10, I describe how my early-career research in Denmark led me to cultivate an interest in "labour lore" as well as labour law. I ought to have realized then (but didn't) that it is precisely lore – unwritten, implicit, informal norms – that makes it so difficult for us to comprehend how labour law actually functions in other countries. Lore, after all, is shaped by complex forces, including history, culture, politics, economics, demography, and geography. How else to explain the response of a Danish employer representative to my question about how industrial disputes are resolved in the absence of legislation governing strikes in that country? "Meet me tomorrow for lunch at Tivoli Gardens," he proposed. When we met the next day, I renewed my enquiry. "*This* is how we resolve disputes," he said, waving his arms across our beer mugs to encompass the crowd of diners engaged in earnest and amicable conversations. "We sit down in Tivoli and talk things through." Whether what he said was strictly true then, I am not sure – although at that point, Denmark had not experienced an official strike in over twenty-five years. I envied the Danes and the Swedes, whose system shared some of these voluntarist characteristics; so did many 1960s-era Canadian scholars and policy-makers. We wanted to flatter the Scandinavians by imitating them, but we had no Tivoli, nor was it likely that we could conjure one up out of thin air. Nonetheless, inspired by the apparent success of the Scandinavian model, a few years later I did recommend that we do the next best thing, that we mandate labour and management to adopt a framework agreement to deal with public-interest labour disputes, an agreement that would be blessed by the state but substantially designed and operated by the other two stakeholders.[11]

Ironically, my next foray into Scandinavian labour law came in 1975, when I was asked on very short notice to address a delegation of Swedish labour experts using the University of California at Los Angeles as a neutral venue to discuss a controversial draft statute designed to radically realign the process of dispute settlement in Swedish workplaces. My skeptical but slightly ribald remarks elicited good-natured responses; they were translated and published in Sweden; and the statute in question (no thanks to me) was

unanimously adopted by the Swedish parliament.[12] This marked the
end of my modest involvement in Scandinavian labour law, and perhaps the beginning of the end of corporatist labour policy in Sweden
and Denmark. *Sic transit Gloria Tivoli.*

However, my interest in comparative labour law and lore more
generally persisted through two crises in the field, to each of which
I was an interested spectator. The first was the enactment of the
Industrial Relations Act 1971, which (crudely put) sought to export
Wagner-style collective bargaining from its home in North America
to the United Kingdom. The act was denounced on policy grounds by
Bill Wedderburn and other labour law experts and was condemned
by Kahn-Freund (a leading scholar of both comparative law and
labour law) as a misguided attempt to "transplant" legislation from
one country to another. Such transplants, he warned, would almost
certainly fail. Given the historical, political, and cultural specific-
ity of national labour laws, he argued, they were unlikely to flourish, or even survive, in a new environment. I tended to agree with
Wedderburn, Kahn-Freund, et al., and was embarrassed to find that
the author of the new law, Geoffrey Howe, had at some point mentioned my contribution to its conception – a briefing on Canadian
labour law I had provided him a year or two earlier.

The second was the difficulty encountered by a group of distinguished labour scholars who undertook through the 1970s to
produce a comparative study of employment contracts, dispute settlement, and other aspects of labour law in six advanced economies.
As they acknowledged at the time, and as subsequent assessments
confirmed, while comparing labour law on the books was hard
enough, comparing labour law in practice was well-nigh impossible.[13] My contribution to a *post mortem* on the project some thirty
years later made the additional point that the advent of globalization
required that comparitivists rethink their state-centric approach:
"the new focus of comparative labor studies," I predicted, "will be
on 'law without the state,' on nonstate and supra-state systems."[14]
Notwithstanding these difficulties, I remained interested in the project of comparative labour law, an interest that only intensified after
I was asked to review Daniel Rodgers's brilliant account of how
America and Europe had exchanged ideas about progressive labour
and social policies for decades, and how the "intellectual economy
of catastrophe" ultimately made these ideas invaluable in constructing America's response to the Great Depression.[15]

In the end, however, I knew that I had to practise what I had preached – to embark on my own comparative project rather than comment on the efforts of others. In 2010, Katherine Stone and I launched an international study of responses to the demise of the "standard contract of employment" – the implicit understanding, widely shared during the postwar era, that employment would constitute a long-term relationship providing employers with a skilled and loyal workforce, workers with decent wages, benefits, and opportunities for advancement, and governments with a platform from which to deliver social programs such as pensions and health insurance. That tacit understanding, we believed and statistics confirmed, was being abandoned by employers in many advanced economies because they preferred more flexible arrangements. We asked fifteen scholars from several academic disciplines and ten countries to provide us with case studies that would reveal how public and private actors – governments and courts, unions and employers – were dealing with the ensuing dislocations. Clearly this was not a conventional project of comparative labour law. One could hardly "compare" Danish labour market "flexicurity" with (say) policies on maternity leave in Spain, or the informal resolution of workplace disputes in the US with labour standards enforcement in Australian supply-chains. Why, then, embark on such a "comparative" project? As I argued in the final essay in our 2013 volume,

> The ultimate ambition of this volume is not merely to afford
> readers new perspectives on their own systems of labour market
> regulation, nor to identify features commonly found in other
> systems, nor to lay the conceptual foundations of a system of
> transnational labour law – though it is all those things as well. It
> is above all to remind ourselves, and ultimately to persuade read-
> ers, of two things: first, that changes in the employment relation
> may require root-and-branch reconstruction of labour market
> regulation and labour law; and second, that cross-national learn-
> ing can play an important role in the process of reconstruction.[16]

All of the contributors felt that the project had been a significant learning experience, the volume was well-reviewed and is cited with some frequency, but the "green shoots" of new labour market strategies we hoped to expose to comparative analysis, and the process of reconstruction we hoped to support, have yet to appear.

The Black Arts of Academic Administration

A significant part of my academic life has been spent, one way or another, in administration. An off-putting word, "administration": one that conjures up images of dull committee meetings, dreary routines and rituals, and the dismal business of getting, spending, and accounting for money. It can be any of the above, of course, and often is. However, in my lexicon and in my life, academic administration has had quite different connotations.

I have always understood administration to be inextricably linked to politics, and politics to the ambition of putting things to rights in the world. As a student politician, for example, I embarked on various quixotic "administrative" campaigns, including one to deny student council funding to the "Six Year Club" of dim-witted football players who had failed to graduate from high school in the then-normal five years and then, later, to mobilize the so-called Students' Administrative Council to press an initially resistant University of Toronto to welcome student refugees from Hungary's ill-fated 1956 uprising. As a very junior academic and self-appointed co-ordinator of the law school's move to York University, as described in chapter 5, I worked with considerable intensity and gratifying success on a far more complex and consequential project. But my official career as an academic administrator began when I became Ogoode's associate dean in January 1968.

Here are some of the files for which I had significant or full responsibility: implementation of the affiliation agreement between York and the Law Society, including the actual physical move to York;[1] reform of the curriculum; development of admissions policies and student evaluation procedures; oversight of the graduate program; the recruitment, care, and feeding of faculty members; faculty governance, including relations with student organizations; and relations with the university senate. Obviously, other colleagues undertook initiatives, contributed ideas, chaired and staffed committees, and, through Faculty Council, had the final say on many issues. Obviously, too, my dean – the charismatic Gerald Le Dain[2] – had ultimate moral and legal responsibility for many of the issues on which I worked. But for much of his deanship, he was simultaneously chairing the high-profile Royal Commission on the Non-Medical Use of Drugs, and consequently he relied to an unusual extent on my advice and assistance.

In effect, I was given a leading role in the re-invention of Canada's largest common law school, and thereby, an opportunity to influence significantly the future course of Canadian legal education. And what an opportunity it was: freed from the conservative influence of our previous governing body, the Law Society; in a new university committed to inter-disciplinarity and social justice; with access to public resources greater than Ontario universities had ever received before (or, arguably, since); and in that "sixties" moment when all institutions were being challenged to reinvent themselves!

Ironically, my own deanship (1972–77) turned out to be a period of diminished achievement, if not actual retrenchment. The exuberant "sixties" mood in higher education subsided after the petro-crisis of 1973; York University experienced a series of governance and financial crises which affected the law school's budget and, to an extent, siphoned off my own energies;[3] the Osgoode community's appetite for change was seemingly sated and it became increasingly difficult to engage my colleagues in significant new initiatives. We also became victims of our own success as other Canadian law faculties adopted measures that we had pioneered, thus diluting our brand as an innovative institution. And worse yet, leading Osgoode scholars were lured away by law firms and other universities, and by judicial and governmental appointments which disrupted promising projects of teaching and research that they had launched as members of our faculty.[4]

I therefore found myself more engaged in unproductive decanal activities than I had anticipated or wished. For example, I had to fight off an attempt by the Law Society to reclaim the name "Osgoode Hall," a mark of the Society's exasperation at what some leading lawyers perceived as our radical tendencies in pedagogy and scholarship. (I was accompanied to my meeting with the Law Society on this subject by York's acting president on his first day in office; at the end of that day he resigned, citing concern about the effect of stress on his health.) More proactively, I organized a series of lunch meetings with leading figures of the bench and bar in an attempt to win their confidence and support. "You may not agree with what we're doing," I argued, "but you should at least understand it." Most of our guests seemed to agree; attempts to interfere with our new approach to legal education diminished and towards the end of my deanship, I was able to launch Osgoode's first-ever financial campaign: a campaign whose results were modest but, all things considered, not disgraceful. My greatest challenge was to sustain morale and momentum within the law school community. I became infamous for proclaiming that Osgoode was "the best law school in the Commonwealth" (as I honestly believed) and mildly unpopular with my colleagues for pressing them to earn that reputation by maintaining the pace of innovation that had characterized our rise to preeminence during the sixties.

I also focused on mobilizing student support for several reasons: to avoid disputes between students and faculty on issues such as curriculum reform and faculty appointments, to ensure that students would remain loyal to the law school after they graduated, and above all, to ensure that their law school experience was both happy and stimulating. Some of my tactics amounted, admittedly, to nothing more than conventional retail politics. I initiated, and faithfully attended, a daily coffee-break in the school's central mixing space, so that I could mingle informally with students and faculty. I wrote a weekly column in the student newspaper – a blog *avant l'internet* – and instituted an annual "Dean for a Day" contest. And I attended as many student events as I could. These tactics were deployed in aid of my primary strategy of treating students seriously and engaging with them substantively on both intellectual and institutional issues. My ultimate aim was to ensure that our sometimes risk-averse and conservative students not only acquiesced in the great pedagogic experiment that Osgoode had launched but became its enthusiastic supporters. Without such support, the experiment could not hope to achieve the transformative effects on the bar and the legal system that we aspired to.

In fact, we greatly underestimated the capacity of traditional legal institutions, patterns of practice, and professional culture to resist the reforming influence of innovative education and scholarship. Or perhaps we overestimated the extent and intensity of the changes in curriculum, pedagogy, and intellectual perspectives that we adopted when Osgoode reinvented itself at York University in the late 1960s and early 1970s. Or perhaps (as Mao Zedong reportedly said of the French revolution), it is still too soon to tell.

Two years after the end of my deanship, in 1979, I was asked by the SSHRC to chair the Consultative Group on Research and Education in Law, the first-ever national study of these subjects. This presented me with an opportunity – rare for an academic administrator – to conduct a post-mortem on an educational experiment he himself had helped to design and execute. The results of this inquiry are summarized in chapter 9. For present purposes, I note only that our report was partly a *mea culpa*, partly a recipe for doing better next time. But how to do better? As I acknowledged in an article some years later, most institutions are shaped by developments in the surrounding political economy and society.[5] This insight became highly relevant in my next administrative incarnation as president of York University.

Two formal, institutional histories of my presidency have been published elsewhere – one written by York's official historian, one by me and my presidential predecessors and successors.[6] In this chapter, I will focus more on my personal experiences as a senior administrator. As I argued at the beginning of this chapter, the whole point of being an academic administrator is to make your corner of the world – your department, your faculty, your university – a better place than it used to be. That's not something that you can accomplish from the top down, which is why I don't like to refer to university presidents as "CEOs" and why the deployment of "management" strategies in an academic context seldom produces the desired results. Not that management strategies always succeed in a business context either: as I proposed in one of my more successful public talks, "businesses should become more university-like," given that universities have had a thousand years of experience as communities of "knowledge workers."[7] And not that certain university functions – purchasing, parking, pensions – don't require the same skills as comparable activities in profit-making enterprises; they must get value for money, satisfy "customers," and meet financial obligations. But, I'm convinced, academic institutions must be organized, governed, and administered in ways that reflect their unique mission: the preservation, creation, critique, and dissemination of knowledge. This mission does much to explain their odd hierarchies and convoluted decision-making processes, their strange rituals and reward systems, and their sometimes disputatious relations with governments, business, and the community more generally.

My view of the university's academic mission is shared by most academics, by many students, and even by the white- and blue-collar staff that processes the university's paperwork and cleans its corridors. It is therefore not only proper but politically expedient for academic administrators to publicly embrace the university's unique knowledge-based mission, and to adhere to it as the central principle guiding their work. Otherwise, they will find themselves at odds with their institution and its many constituencies. I made my own commitment to academic excellence explicit in my installation address (delivered, not by coincidence, on my fiftieth birthday), and hewed to it pretty conscientiously in the way I spoke and behaved in private and in public, in making appointments and approving promotions, in framing institutional plans and priorities, and in allocating scarce institutional resources. In general, I think this earned me a fair degree of goodwill.

However, this commitment also led me into what I referred to above as "disputatious relations" with government. I began my term as president on 1 January 1985, in the dying days of a forty-year-old Conservative government that was committed, in an odious ministerial phrase, to ensuring "more scholar for the dollar." Six months into my presidency a minority Liberal government took office, supported by an electoral pact with the NDP. The new minister for colleges and universities was Gregory Sorbara, a former student of mine at Osgoode and, as he declared on his first day in office, a firm believer in liberal education. Sorbara also believed in fairness. With the premier's backing, he launched a review of the funding formula which, under the Conservatives, had discriminated against new, expanding universities like York while favouring older "research intensive" institutions like Toronto. We made a strong case to the advisory body conducting the review, the Ontario Council on University Affairs, which in turn recommended a fair and sensible new formula to the government – not everything we asked for, but fair and sensible. However, to my consternation, the University of Toronto and a small coalition of its spear-carriers and fellow-travellers mounted a clandestine, but successful, effort to persuade the government to re-jig the OCUA's recommendations to York's severe prejudice. When the results were announced I was apoplectic but, after due consideration, decided to console myself with the government's offer to fund a badly needed new Fine Arts building at York.

In due course, the Liberals were re-elected with a majority, and our relations ran relatively smoothly for the rest of their mandate. However, the election of 1990 brought to power Ontario's first NDP government. Rather surprisingly, our relations with the new minister for colleges and universities (an academic historian by trade) proved to be extremely difficult. In part, this was because the NDP government was experiencing severe financial pressures, to which it responded with severe austerity measures – the infamous "social contract" of 1992 – that ultimately sealed its fate. In part, too, tensions arose when the government (or at least the minister's political advisors) gave priority to its equity program. This program – to which we wholeheartedly subscribed – diverted energies, goodwill, and material resources from other worthy causes such as funding our under-resourced academic activities. Finally, a significant point of tension was the minister's ill-concealed antipathy towards university administrators, myself included. Perhaps this antipathy arose out of his own experience in academe; perhaps it was a pose adopted to satisfy campus groups with their own agendas; perhaps my fellow presidents and I provoked and deserved it. Thankfully I retired as president in 1992, just as the social contract was taking hold, and consequently never did learn why our relations with the government had deteriorated so badly.

York had (and still has) a strongly egalitarian culture, and my emphasis on excellence was opposed in some circles on ideological grounds. I'm afraid, too, that I gave short shrift to our intercollegiate athletics programs, which seemed to consume considerable resources while contributing little to our academic mission. And, of course, I could not escape the inevitable and controversial trade-offs between (say) increasing salaries across the board (as proposed by the faculty union) and using those same dollars to launch new programs, increase the faculty complement, or support outstanding scholars (all objectives favoured by members of the faculty union in their capacity as members of the academic senate).

I adopted a four-fold strategy to resolve these difficulties. First, through my active participation in the academic planning process, I tried to persuade my fellow senators to adopt policies that would ratchet up our ambitions, performance, and reputation. I was largely successful in this approach because I was well-briefed, willing to make compromises, and formally on record as being prepared to "put my money where my mouth is," to make budget allocations in support of the priorities identified by the collegium. Second, I engaged directly, frequently, and substantively with all of the university's constituencies – unions, student organizations, faculty, and departmental councils – in a series of open meetings. When particularly intense criticisms were voiced by individuals at these meetings, I made it my business to meet with them one-on-one, to hear them out and to explain my own position. This did not necessarily change anyone's mind, but at least it convinced most people that I was not acting arbitrarily. Most people, but not all: following a dispute over the rearrangement of faculty offices, I received a stiff note from one displaced occupant accusing me of being an "agent of hegemonic capitalism." My staff promptly presented me with a T-shirt bearing that motto. I treasure it still, and for its part hegemonic capitalism has apparently flourished despite its serious error of judgment in selecting me as its agent.

Secondly, I worked hard to improve York's resources, so that not every decision would involve zero-sum financial choices. Our briefs to OCUA (which advised the government on funding issues) were well-researched, and as convincingly and passionately argued as I could make them. I appointed a vice-president whose mandate included fundraising in the private sector and lobbying government on York's behalf, as well as community and alumni relations. I established York University Development Company to implement a strategy of converting the university's surplus lands into capital that we could use to reconfigure our barren campus, build buildings to accommodate our constantly expanding academic activities and, for the first time, provide the York community with decent amenities. Over the course of my presidency, YUDC produced a new campus master plan, built some $200 million worth of buildings, and materially improved both academic and social life on campus.

Third, I organized a series of external alliances to support York in its search for a fair share of government funding, and for a policy environment in which the interests of emerging universities like ours would be protected from the depredations of older and more prestigious institutions. These alliances included coordination with like-minded universities, a cross-party caucus of provincial legislators with York connections, cultivation of the major ethnic groups represented amongst York's students, and the establishment of a satellite campus in a nearby community that housed a dense collection of high-tech businesses.

And finally, I intervened directly to improve York's academic reputation and performance. This involved the development of a strong academic planning process, the close monitoring of appointments and promotion and tenure decisions, and the strategic deployment of resources to support both worthy new initiatives and established high-performing academic units. By the end of my term as president, the number and quality of undergraduate and graduate applicants to York had improved considerably, our grants from federal research funding agencies rose very significantly, and we had become a more diverse community – both demographically and academically – than we had previously been.

While many aspects of my strategy paid off, others were less successful. But overall, they helped to alleviate our financial problems, generated a sense of momentum within the university, largely dispelled the pessimism and perversity that constant cutbacks had produced within the faculty, and helped to persuade the public, and the government, that York was a cause worth supporting. A far cry from advancing academic values, one might say – but perhaps not so far. I was deeply impressed with a graffito I had stumbled on in London just before I began my presidency: "The Economy Is the Secret Police of Our Desires." To gratify York's academic desires, we had first to neutralize the "secret police," to get hold of the necessary resources. That is what my four-pronged strategy sought to accomplish.

This strategy advanced academic values in another respect as well: in my own future as a scholar. Immersion in a wide variety of political manoeuvres, in land development, and in the management of a complex institution turned out to be a wonderful learning experience for me. I began my presidency as a slightly unorthodox public and labour lawyer; I ended it with a relatively sophisticated understanding of higher education policy and public policy more generally, and thereby became the "useful idiot" described in chapter 9.

My years as president also transformed me intellectually in other ways. Presidents are inevitably exposed to academic vernaculars, to intellectual traditions, other than their own. I am not an historian, an economist, or a space scientist. Nonetheless I had to read the promotion files of historians, open conferences on economics, and advocate the cause of space scientists seeking government support for a research centre. In order to do these things effectively, I had to understand a little about their discipline – not much, perhaps, but at least enough to allow me to make some assessment of the significance of their work and to avoid sounding stupid in public or private discussions. Seven-plus years of living "outside the law" in the company of intelligent people anxious to educate me in their particular ways of thinking subtly detached me from my own law-yerly thought-patterns and allowed me to return to the legal acad-emy with broader perspectives than I had when I left it to become president. And a good thing that was: the years of my presidency were years of great change in law and legal thought. To cite but one example, the Supreme Court had decided virtually no Charter cases when I became president in January 1985, but when I returned to academic life in July 1992, there were scores of decisions on the books. I was able to view them with more detachment than I would have had if I had been closely following developments and, conse-quently, was inspired some years later to write an article, mentioned previously, that asked "Does the Charter Matter?"[8]

Of course, my presidential experience was also shaped by the intellectual tools I brought to the job. A case in point: within a few weeks of beginning my term, I was asked to approve the expulsion of a student who had been found guilty of sexual harassment by a senior university administrator. On reviewing the file, I realized that our procedures for rusticating students were seriously defective – so much so that they were unlikely to survive judicial scrutiny. Using my knowledge of administrative and labour law, and drawing on my recent work on legal pluralism, I spent the next weekend design-ing a system of student discipline that served York well for many years. In short, to reframe Clauswitz's famous aphorism about war ("the continuation of diplomacy by other means"), for me university administration was the continuation of scholarship by other means.

But not only scholarship – it was a series of life lessons in human frailty and perversity. Some humorous examples first. My presidency got off to a soggy start; at the formal luncheon before my installa-tion, an inexperienced student server managed to pour Cumberland sauce down my suit jacket rather than onto my plate; fortunately, I wore a gown during the ceremony, so no one was the wiser. A fac-ulty member asked if I could perform marriages like the captain of a ship; I was sorely tempted to do so (if things didn't work out, both parties would be grateful they weren't really married) but I declined. A deranged, elderly physician snuck through my back garden and into my kitchen one day; she offered to arrange the transfer of the University of Toronto medical school to our university if only I would guarantee that no "orientals" would be admitted, and that York would reinstate her son, who had failed his exams; she refused to leave until I picked up the phone and began to dial for police assistance. And some not so humorous examples next. The morning after a highly confidential meeting of our board to discuss a major equipment purchase, I arrived at my office to find the president of an unsuccessful bidder ensconced in the waiting room; clearly, someone at the meeting had tipped him off. As part of our new, transparent academic planning process, I invited a key campus union to a meeting to provide its input on budget priorities; my administrative colleagues and I sat twiddling our thumbs for half an hour before someone advised us that the union had simply decided neither to attend nor to tell us that they weren't coming. After leading a delegation to seek better funding for Ontario's universities, I was called aside by the minister whom we were importuning; he advised me that his daughter had been sexually harassed by a York professor, and that just that morning he had learned that the daughter of a cabinet colleague had been harassed by the same professor; fortunately, the harasser was only a few weeks from retirement, but he remained on the payroll long enough to receive a well-deserved reprimand. Bottom line: I think I somehow managed to keep on "the high road" while responding to difficult situations with humour or tough responses, as required.

This relatively positive account of my presidential years may surprise those who are used to thinking of universities in general (and York in particular) as communities in turmoil. Why have I said nothing about the campus wars over the Israel-Palestine conflict? Why have I failed to acknowledge that universities have been degraded, intellectually and morally, by so-called political correctness? Why have I ignored the corporatization of our institutions, their capture by business-type values, procedures, and leadership? The answer is simple: none of these issues came to a boil during my watch.

True, I would have welcomed more opportunities to resist corporate temptation. However, whatever its shortcomings, Canadian capitalism was not so stupid as to waste its time or money on subverting York's faculty or students, both of whom were notoriously – if somewhat inaccurately – identified as deep-dyed leftists. But how would I have responded to student militancy, political correctness, or attempts by rival groups to ban each other from campus? Poorly, I suspect, as I hold a number of beliefs that are not necessarily widely shared these days.

I am deeply committed to the notion that universities exist primarily to promote liberal learning[9] (but if they also promote economic growth and/or social justice, so much the better). Second, as a corollary of my first proposition, they must regard academic freedom as their most important value (but they must be prepared to live with the inevitable controversies). Third, it is not the function of universities to ensure that people feel "safe" or "secure" in their values and beliefs – rather the contrary (but of course their physical safety must be carefully guarded). And finally, so long as access to higher education and academic careers remains a scarce commodity, intellectual capacity to benefit from and contribute to the university's mission seems the only fair criterion by which to ration access (but in measuring "capacity," the distorting effects of discrimination on grounds of class, ethnicity, religion, disability, and gender must be eliminated).

In short, I doubt that, despite the best efforts of university administrators, it will ever be possible to strike precisely the right balance between social justice and equity, on the one hand, and academic values such as excellence on the other. For example, I would resist the so-called "heckler's veto" that is used to ensure that no one on campus will be exposed to views they find offensive, while at the same time I would use the "bully pulpit" of my presidency to defend vulnerable groups and my control of the budget to fund recruitment initiatives, establish teaching programs, and sponsor research that advanced their cause. This approach might well prove unacceptable to many campus groups, and if I espoused them as president today, I would almost certainly find myself in trouble. However, I do believe that the best we can realistically hope for is to keep moving in the right direction even if, at any given moment, that movement seems to have slowed or even reversed. Along the way there will be controversies and crises, as there rightly should be. Injustice will never cease of its own accord, nor can it be overcome without forcing universities and their presidents to confront difficult choices. That is why I believe it is a president's duty to try to persuade people with opposing views to listen to each other, to confront prejudice head-on, to meet hateful speech with vigorous rebuttals (including those of the president him- or herself), and to take practical measures to sweep away cultural, structural, and procedural barriers to substantive fairness for everyone.

"Evasion and arm-waving," skeptical readers will say, "self-serving platitudes." Maybe so, but here is some evidence that I mean what I say, for whatever that is worth.

As a young academic in the late 1960s, I appeared before a parliamentary committee to defend freedom of expression by opposing legislation criminalizing "hate speech." As dean, I helped to establish Osgoode's equity admissions program, which afforded applicants the chance to demonstrate by means other than their LSAT and GPA scores that they had the ability to handle law studies, launched our admissions officer on a proactive campaign to recruit potential equity candidates, and hired a special teaching assistant to help these students meet the challenges of law school. (I became critical of the program when our Admissions Committee declined to evaluate the success of our alternative screening procedures.) I also recruited Osgoode's first female faculty members – Louise Arbour as a tenure-track assistant professor, and Judy LaMarsh as a visiting professor. Subsequently, as president, I appointed a number of able women to senior administrative posts and devised a system of subsidies to encourage academic units to improve the gender balance of their faculty. However, my record is not without blemish. I rejected a female candidate for the Osgoode deanship (a sometime personal friend, as it happened) in favour of a male, the search committee's preferred candidate, because she had a reputation for bureaucratic behaviour and because she declined to discuss the current state of the law school with me or to suggest how she thought it might be improved. (Not one female faculty member at York supported the resulting human rights complaint, which was ultimately settled by the university's commitment to establish an Institute for Feminist Legal Studies, a highly desirable move on its own merits and without regard to the controversy.)

Another bit of evidence that may or may not persuade sceptics: I once intercepted a student group *en route* to occupying my office with the aim of forcing York to divest its financial holdings in apartheid-era South Africa. "You're too late," I said. "My office has already been occupied by someone who favours divestment. Me. York has nothing to divest." We all held hands and sang "We Shall Overcome." (Some months earlier, I had instructed the relevant university official to quietly get rid of our South African holdings and had persuaded Ontario's then-attorney general to amend the Trustee Act in order to enable our pension fund to do likewise without fear of legal reprisal by its beneficiaries.)

Of course, I was not able to devote all of my time to issues of grand strategy, high policy, and moral complexity. Universities are not just knowledge factories where people teach, study, and conduct research. They are also complex communities where people live and work, where they park their cars and eat lunch, and where, unfortunately, they may exhibit idiosyncratic, self-regarding, and erratic behaviours that do not necessarily contribute to – and occasionally detract from – the university's academic mission. And they are communities where people (especially faculty members) are clever, articulate, empowered, and embedded for years and decades, if not lifetimes. Inevitably, some part of my job was to deal with the undeniable fact that people are only human. To set the mood, I decreed that members of the president's staff must willingly suspend disbelief and assume that everyone was acting in good faith and in the best interests of the university, as they inevitably claimed they were. Suspending disbelief, however, was not always easy. While most people behaved sensibly and decently most of the time, my staff and I witnessed instances of self-dealing, grudge-settling, favouritism, gross misjudgment, and general clueless-ness. Despite having suspended disbelief, I ultimately had to confront several people about their failings, take appropriate remedial or puni-tive action, and, in a very few cases, terminate their tenure in office or their relationship with York. I always did so with regret, and a sense that "there but for the grace of God go I."

Administrative service can generate turmoil in the personal and professional lives of the people who engage in it. The work is end-less and often emotionally draining, so friendships and family rela-tionships can be placed under stress; there is a lingering fear that academics become intellectually "rusty" after too many years away from the lab bench or the library, so they cling to administrative office rather than return to professorial status; temptations for self-aggrandizement can erode the academic values of even highly principled administrators; and rightly or wrongly, scholars who take on administrative responsibilities are often accused by colleagues of having gone over to the dark side – an accusation that makes some of them cynical, and thus becomes a self-fulfilling prophecy.

Of course, it is easier to see these things happening to others than it is to detect them in one's self. However, my own assessment is that

I came out of my presidency no worse a person than I was when I entered it, and arguably a better one. This would not be entirely surprising. After all, as a French philosopher has observed, "many a person becomes good by leading a life of hypocrisy" – a not inapt description of much presidential behaviour.

8

Adventures in Pedagogy

Over my forty-plus years as a legal academic, I had a lot to say about the governance, curricula, and scholarly cultures of law schools, but relatively little to say about what actually goes on in the classroom – a point astutely noted by a friendly commentator on my work on legal education.[1] In this chapter, I hope to make amends for my neglect of this important subject by recounting some of my adventures in pedagogy.

To begin somewhere around the middle of my career: a student in labour law intervened in a class discussion one day to say, "I'm sick and tired of hearing how stupid judges are and how clever law professors are." This prompted a rejoinder from another student: "Listen you," she said, "This is the best class in the best course I have ever taken in all my years of university. If you don't like it, you can f*** off." He did; I never saw him again.

What to make of this exchange?

The most obvious conclusion is that one can't please all of one's students all the time. That said, my end-of-term evaluations were usually pretty positive, though I never did win a teaching award. Second, if nothing else, my classes sometimes generated controversy – as indeed they were bound to do. Labour and administrative law, my two main fields of teaching, were concerned with controversial issues on which opinions in the class (as in the wider society) differed widely. Third, one might infer from the disgruntled student's comment that I showed a lack of respect for judges and, more generally, for conventional wisdom and its proprietors and proponents. Guilty as charged. I believed, and I taught, that judicial pronouncements were often poorly reasoned and/or likely to lead to undesirable or impractical outcomes. But if guilty, I also plead in mitigation that measured disrespect (mine was always measured!) was part of my job description. How else to sharpen my students' critical faculties or make them understand that legal disputes have long-term, societal consequences? How else to move the law ahead and promote thoughtful debate about good public policy?

What does this say about my teaching technique? To answer that question, I have to take a step back to describe the evolution of law school pedagogy over the course of my career.

As in many other disciplines, the magisterial style of teaching – the set-piece fifty-minute lecture – prevailed in most Canadian law schools until well into the twentieth century. It had its advantages: a professor could develop an "authoritative" account of "The Law of X," provide students with instructions on when and how to invoke "The Law," and efficiently test their mastery of the subject by asking them to solve a hypothetical legal problem. But also its disadvantages: "The Law of X" was almost always a messy work-in-progress, not a determinate body of inflexible rules; students could no more learn how to use legal rules by passively listening to lectures than they could learn to swim if instructed in the same fashion; and solutions generated by simply applying what passed for the authoritative version of "The Law" would not necessarily serve the best interests of either clients or society.

By the 1960s, in many law schools (at the University of Toronto, but not yet at Osgoode) magisterial lectures had been largely replaced by the so-called "Socratic" or "case" method. Developed at Harvard Law School in the 1870s, the case method had many variants. Essentially, professors assigned students several judicial decisions to read before class. In different versions of the case method, students would then be asked in the context of a classroom discussion to evaluate the relative merits of contradictory precedents, to use the assigned materials to resolve hypothetical disputes, or to consider how the law might be changed in order to produce clearer rules and better outcomes.

I adopted the case method when I first began teaching, although hardly any of my Osgoode colleagues used it. I reckoned that it would force students to recognize law's indeterminacy and encourage scepticism about judicial authority; it would hone students' analytical and advocacy skills; and best of all, it would ensure that they assumed some responsibility for their own learning experience. However, that is not how the case method necessarily worked in practice. Many students dreaded being called on in class. When they were, they sometimes pretended that they were not present (a workable strategy in large classes), claimed that they had not had a chance to read the assigned materials, bluffed their way through a dialogue for which they were clearly unprepared, or simply failed to hold up their end of the conversation, forcing me to conduct a Socratic dialogue with myself. At the other extreme, a few students intervened too aggressively and too frequently in class discussions, whether to win my approval, to hone their skills, or simply to assert their dominance; understandably, they aroused the ire of their less assertive colleagues.

All in all, I soon acquired doubts about the case method which, whatever its virtues, contributed to an atmosphere of embarrassment, intimidation, and ill-will in the classroom. Those doubts crystallized one day in the late sixties when I called upon an unprepared student and he looked up at me in sheer terror, jets of blood spurting from his nose. I decided there and then to pretty much abandon Socratic dialogue. In fact, I had already become disillusioned with the case method, not because of its baleful impact on students' psyches or blood pressure but because of its pedagogic shortcomings. It simply did not allow me to pursue the broad agenda of issues with which I hoped to engage my students.

This did not matter much in the traditional first-year, black-letter courses – Personal Property and Contracts – which I taught only briefly and in which I had no particular intellectual investment. But it did very much matter in the public law subjects which I was not only teaching but (I hoped) re-inventing at the same time. I wanted students to get a feel for the real-life tensions of labour-management relations; I wanted them to understand that administrative regimes were established to deliver effective protection to disempowered citizens; I wanted them to understand that public law in general involved choices that were clearly political. However, appellate judgments – the building blocks of the case method – tended to filter out the drama of workplace conflict and compromise, to portray administrative agencies as illicit derogations from the rule of law, and to obfuscate the ideological dimension of the controversies that they were meant to resolve. Clearly I had to replace, or at least significantly supplement, the case method, if I was to achieve my teaching objectives.

I got off to a good start. In my first-ever class in labour law, I screened a docudrama that took students through the events leading up to, and during, a strike. As the years went on, I sought new ways to expose my students to the drama of labour law, whether real or simulated. I involved them in mock parliamentary debates over legislation designed to limit union rights, and in simulated negotiation and mediation exercises. I invited practitioners to tell "war stories" about the joys and perils of representing workers or employers (and added a few of my own drawn from my experience as a labour neutral and policy advisor). I challenged students to resolve the practical, ethical, and legal problems I planted in the ongoing narrative of a fictitious labour-management relationship that accompanied the assigned readings. And of course, in order to incite vigorous class discussions, I always offered commentary designed to place those readings in a broader social and political context, and to provide a robust critique of judicial pronouncements that were poorly reasoned or insensitive to the dynamic of industrial relations.[2]

In administrative law, I confess, my teaching technique was less adventurous. This reflected the greater complexity of the systemic critique I was trying to deliver and the absence of teachable materials with which to make my point, as well as, perhaps, a failure of imagination on my part. How does one get students to immerse themselves in, say, the technical and political complexities of land use regulation or the administration of prison discipline? One fairly successful technique involved asking them to supplement the facts provided in the judgments I assigned for reading with additional "probable facts" they might be able to conjure up from their general knowledge or educated guesses. An example: courses in administrative law often introduce students early on to the case of *Cooper v Wandsworth*,[3] an 1863 English decision that helped to establish the point that even if their governing statute is silent on the matter, administrative decision-makers must provide "natural justice" – essentially a fair hearing – to the people whose conduct they are regulating. The Wandsworth Board of Works pulled down a house that Cooper was constructing because he had failed to file his plans and obtain the necessary permit, without giving him either notice or an opportunity to argue against this action. "Why," I asked my students, "would the board have done such a thing? Perhaps the answer is a seven-letter word." I then offered to buy coffee for anyone who guessed that word. No one ever did.

The word, I maintained, was "cholera." London had experienced recurring bouts of the disease, but only beginning in the 1850s did it require sanitation systems to be installed that separated clean drinking water from bacteria-laden sewage. By constructing the house without first filing plans, Cooper (an experienced builder) had made it impossible for the board to determine whether he had complied with the new sanitary arrangements. All this was conjecture, of course; but it was the kind of conjecture I wanted students to train themselves to undertake. This approach, I hoped, would inoculate them against the prevailing tendency amongst administrative lawyers to invoke vague concepts like "natural justice" while ignoring compelling societal concerns such as public health.

In both labour and administrative law, then, it would be fair to say that I "had an agenda." I was not interested in having students simply learn The Law; I wanted them to understand that The Law was always changing, often obscure, sometimes illogical or unfair, seldom fixed and clear. I wanted them to understand as well that The Law did not exist in a parallel universe, apart from society, the economy, and the polity. And finally, I wanted them to develop their critical faculties, to feel free to criticize either judicial pronouncements or my own commentary on them. Here is how I described my pedagogic ambitions in an article published shortly after my retirement:

[We should] ... engage students in serious conversations which will free them from the tyranny of rules. This requires that we adopt a certain posture in the classroom. First, we must give students confidence that their experience of family and school and their encounters with people, culture and work is somehow relevant to their legal studies. This will provide them with a vantage point from which to begin to question the wisdom dispensed by judges, legal texts and ourselves. Second, we have to convince them that despite our own comprehensive knowledge of law, sociology, philosophy, politics, economics, history, astrology, sport and sex, we still value questions more than answers. Third, we must show them how to use their newfound confidence not just to challenge the instructor and interrogate the materials being taught, but to dare to ask questions of themselves. And finally, we must help them get used to the fact that they are embarking on a course of study, and ultimately on a career, that will require them to live at ease with multiple truths, irresolvable conflicts, abundant ambiguities and ironies galore.[4]

This approach, I confess, did not always sit well with my own students. Not only did my approach require them to invest more effort in preparing for class or consolidating their knowledge afterwards, it left many of them with a sense of insecurity, a fear that their expensive legal education might not, after all, lead to a professional career in which financial and psychological rewards were guaranteed. In some cases, as well, my approach nudged them into reconsidering their own long-held (though not always carefully considered) beliefs about politics, society, and the legal system itself. While I did my best to put students at ease – treating them respectfully, using humour, showing them how to express themselves more effectively – I don't doubt that I left a few of them disconcerted and dissatisfied. At the same time (as ex-students have occasionally reassured me), many did gain a good deal from my teaching. This would be true, of course, for the students with whom I worked most closely on term papers or other individual assignments; but I hope and believe that even those with whom I had less contact came away with ideas and approaches that helped to make them better lawyers, better citizens, and better people.

Graduate supervision is, of course, the most intensive form of teaching, the most carefully individualized, and the most intellectually rigorous. I supervised the second student ever to enrol in Osgoode's Master of Laws (LLM) program in the early 1960s – Warren Winkler, a future chief justice of Ontario. Over the next decade, I supervised another half dozen LLM students (not all of whom were as successful as my first), and on several occasions directed the graduate program and conducted a graduate seminar in legal education. However, only following my return to academe, in 1992, did graduate supervision begin to make significant claims on my time. Because most of my graduate students worked on themes not directly related to my own expertise – such as corporate governance, law and development issues, the domestic reception of international human rights law, and postmodern constitutional theory – I was unable to guide them towards a better understanding of substantive issues in their research. Consequently, I focused on helping them to understand and address the larger implications of their concerns and to improve their analytical abilities and writing styles. I was more than happy to do this because they, in turn, taught me a good deal about subjects I would never have become embroiled with otherwise. I am still co-supervising a doctoral candidate and have no intention of abandoning the field any time soon.

Finally, I think I can fairly claim to have been an advocate and successful practitioner of experiential learning – an approach currently much favoured at Osgoode and elsewhere. Experiential learning involves three elements: "(1) exposure to substantive or procedural legal knowledge; (2) engagement in law-related activity; and (3) the opportunity to reflect on legal experience and its implications for legal ideas."[5] As an advocate of this approach, I was an early supporter of Osgoode's ground-breaking legal clinic, Parkdale Community Legal Services, and as dean aggressively defended it against attempts by the Law Society to prevent its operation.[6] More importantly, in my 1983 report, *Law and Learning*, I argued that law schools should embrace clinical pedagogy and, if they deemed it appropriate, should organize their curricula around that form of teaching.[7] As an "experiential learning" practitioner, my own most ambitious effort was an advanced seminar on "globalization and labour" – in current usage, a "praxicum" – offered in tandem with a similar seminar organized by a colleague at SUNY Buffalo. Students at both schools were provided with background information and assigned roles that required them to work together to negotiate a collective agreement covering auto workers and auto companies on both sides of the border, and then to reflect on the experience. But most of my forays into experiential learning were more modest: as noted, students participated from time to time in simulated negotiations, mediations, and arbitrations; they debated and drafted legislation; they talked to practitioners and observed tribunals in action. My aim was primarily to animate (and/or challenge) the still-life painting of legal rules, institutions, and processes that students take away from conventional course materials. If they also happened to acquire skills and practical knowledge that would help them in their future careers, so much the better.

That said, I had (and still have) reservations about experiential learning. First, to the extent that "experience" involves participation in and observation of everyday legal practice, there is a risk that students will too readily come to accept the values, methods, and outcomes they observe as normal or desirable. Second, while that risk is minimized by the provision of close academic supervision and carefully structured opportunities for informed reflection, providing such safeguards is resource-intensive. Given an overall shortage of resources, some law schools may be tempted to skimp. Third, while no doubt some students learn some things more effectively when they are taught via experiential methods, this type of learning is unlikely to be optimal for all students and all subject matters. And most importantly, as I argued both in *Law and Learning* and subsequently,[8] the greatest shortcoming in the teaching programs of Canadian law schools is not their failure to mobilize experiential learning opportunities that will produce "practice ready" lawyers. It is their inability to provide a supportive environment for students and professors whose current interests and future careers require them to take a critical distance from the legal system and legal practice as we know them today. To sum up: immersion in real or simulated practice situations certainly has many pedagogic attractions, but it does not address what I believe is the most serious gap in the Canadian legal academy. To fill that gap, I have recommended that some law schools should offer at least some of their students a different kind of educational experience, one that focuses on big ideas, that engages closely with adjacent disciplines, and that does not assume that legal practice is the destiny of each and every graduate.

However, while I identify as the most serious shortcoming of our law schools the absence of opportunities for tough, structured, and sustained intellectual engagement, my views are not widely shared. In fact, my advocacy of an intellectually intensive stream in legal education has met with almost total opposition from almost all law teachers at almost every Canadian law school – including those who share my commitment to broadening and deepening the intellectual experience of law students. Moreover, I have to admit that some of my critics have been spectacularly successful in providing their students with just such an experience within the constraints of the current curriculum. Scores of Rod Macdonald's students, for example, have testified to his inspiring and provocative teaching,[9] and testimonials for retiring or deceased legal academics regularly attest to the horizon-broadening influence they have had on their students. I cannot, in all honesty, write such a testimonial on my own behalf. Yes, every now and then, a student intervention in class, an essay, or an exam script has astonished me with its depth and/or daring in a way that seemed to reflect the influence of my teaching, even if only by reacting against it. And yes, some of those astonishing students did go on to brilliant careers in academe or government or civil society rather than in private practice. But just as often they disappeared into productive but humdrum professional lives, while not-so-brilliant students turned out to be the ones who made distinctive contributions to legal thought and public policy, or forged reputations as great judges or awesome advocates. As the depressing two weeks or so I spent each year grading exam papers confirmed, my teaching was not having the transformative effects I hoped it would.

In the end, I decided to give it all up and retire, but it wasn't despair or disappointment that led me to do so. It was the realization that my students and I were inhabiting different intellectual and discursive universes, different psychic spaces and cultures. This was true at many levels. The map of my political world was the map of the world of the 1930s through the 1950s which my own teachers had handed on to me; my understanding of law was shaped by the legal-cultural revolutions I had experienced and helped to shape in the 1960s and 1970s. However, by the 1990s and 2000s, my students were (metaphorically) Thatcher's children and Reagan's. In contrast to my assumption that government exists to protect people from abuses of private power, my students harboured an instinctive mistrust of government, seeing it as either the agent of elites and technocrats or an alien presence that disrupted the natural ordering produced by market forces. Whereas I grew up listening to war bulletins on the radio, my students texted each other on their cell phones or worked their way down musical playlists while sitting in class. My humour, my rhetoric, my metaphors and allusions missed the mark more and more frequently, simply because I wasn't reading what they read, listening to what they listened to, leading the lives they led.

As an undergraduate, I had read *La dernière classe*, a short story by Alphonse Daudet. The year is 1870. A schoolteacher in Alsace – the province France has just lost to an invading Prussian army – is informed that in the future instruction will be conducted in German, not French. As a final gesture of defiance and patriotism, he writes on the blackboard *Vive la France* and disappears from the classroom, presumably forever – a glorious but definitive end to a life given over to pedagogy. I felt a bit like that schoolteacher as I passed a couple of bottles of wine around my own *dernière classe* in 2005.

My Career as a Useful Idiot –
Commissions and Their Consequences

When a government or some other body needs to address an intractable problem, it will often turn to a "useful idiot" – a well-reputed person who can be counted on to study the problem carefully, to write an insightful report, and to make sensible recommendations which can then be safely ignored. I have served as just such a useful idiot on a number of occasions.

Several of these involved institutions of higher learning. In 1972, just before becoming dean of Osgoode, I was asked by the Ontario government to review the administration of the Ontario College of Art (now the Ontario College of Art and Design University). OCA's recently appointed principal – an English artist-educator named Roy Ascott – had arrived with what he understood to be a mandate to shake up what was (in his estimation) a stodgy and unexciting institution.[1] His methods and those of his team were somewhat unorthodox, and included smashing the plaster models used for drawing classes, publicly executing a live chicken, and peremptorily firing a significant proportion of the teaching staff. Chaos ensued. Student enrolments fell dramatically; faculty members who had been dismissed threatened to sue; and the college faced a crisis that was both financial and reputational. The college's governing council and the provincial Ministry of Education wanted to know what to do next. After some weeks of investigation and reflection, I recommended Ascot's removal, the strengthening of the OCA's governance structures and administration, and the reinstatement of its illegally dismissed staff. On this occasion my recommendations were largely implemented, which led me to imagine that future commissions would end as happily.

Some did. A quarter century later, in 1997, with Professor Joyce Lorimer of Wilfrid Laurier University, I co-chaired an inquiry into the administration of Trent University, where almost all of the senior administrators had resigned in the wake of a bitter labour dispute. Looking back, I am almost embarrassed by the banality of our recommendations, which included greater civility amongst members of the university community, better training for senior officials, a clearer definition of their responsibilities, a modest restructuring of Trent's governing bodies, more transparency in its financial affairs, and a determined effort to lay to rest a long-smouldering dispute over the university's pension plan.[2] People at Trent didn't need us to tell them these things. However, what they did need was a "time out" – a pause in the conflict, an opportunity for catharsis, and a reminder that members of the Trent community shared many values, even though sharp differences of opinion – real and imagined, over matters personal and institutional – had poisoned the atmosphere. In due course people at Trent re-discovered the better angels of their nature, and the institution subsequently enjoyed a period of relative peace and progress.

On the other hand, some didn't. By far the most dramatic of my university inquiries took place at Concordia University following the murder of four engineering professors and the wounding of a staff member by a disaffected mathematician, Valery Fabrikant. By the time of the inquiry, Fabrikant had been convicted of murder and was serving a life sentence. However, at his trial and in subsequent communications, he claimed that his actions had been provoked by his failure to receive the tenure-track appointment that he had been promised, allegedly in exchange for writing scientific articles for which his dean would receive unearned credit as co-author. He also claimed that his department chair and the head of his research centre were beneficiaries of similar illicit arrangements. And he maintained that all three had used staff, equipment, and facilities belonging to the university, and funded in part by the Natural Sciences and Engineering Research Council of Canada (NSERC), to advance the business interests of their private consulting firms. I was appointed chair of a committee mandated to investigate Fabrikant's allegations.

To our own dismay and discomfort, our committee – myself and two distinguished scientists, Jon Thompson of the University of New Brunswick and Roger Blais of l'École Polytechnique de Montréal – concluded that Fabrikant's allegations were largely true. Obviously, this finding did not lead us to justify his violent reaction. Rather, we sought to place the underlying situation in a broader context so that Concordia and other institutions could stamp out the undesirable practices that our investigation had revealed. Our report, *Integrity in Scholarship*,[3] therefore focused on what we called "the political economy of scholarship" that prevailed in Concordia's engineering faculty. In that unit, as in much of Canadian academe, rewards in the form of jobs, promotions, honours, grants, and contracts flowed to those who produced the most publications, presented at the greatest number of conferences, and attracted the most lucrative partnerships with private-sector firms. This reward system, we found, provided incentives not only for genuine scholarly achievement, but also for illicit, deceptive, and even fraudulent behaviour. The university, we concluded, had not adopted appropriate arrangements to prevent, detect, or punish such behaviour.

Concordia's board of governors was not pleased with our report. I should have expected this reaction. While we were still drafting our report, the chair of the board and his lawyer insisted on coming to Toronto to see me. What they wanted, it soon became clear, was for us to fix blame for the whole situation on the university's rector, Patrick Kenniff. Their intervention was a clear assault on our committee's independence, guaranteed by its mandate. Moreover, as our report subsequently made clear, we believed that primary responsibility for the situation lay with Concordia's vice-rector (Academic). Worse yet, from the board's perspective, our findings impugned the reputations of three of the university's most prolific scholars, who happened also to be generous donors. And worst of all, the board feared that our findings might be seen as giving moral support to a convicted murderer – though that was certainly not our intention.

In any event, for some weeks after the report was submitted, the board declined to release it – a clear breach of its promise to do so. During this period, I received several letters from the board's lawyer raising spurious objections to our findings and implying that dire consequences would ensue if we insisted on publication – a further violation of the terms of our mandate, under which the university promised to indemnify us in the event that our report should come under legal attack. As my colleagues and I struggled with these developments, the impasse over publication was resolved in an unexpected fashion. I had asked a member of Osgoode's support staff to fax a copy of my correspondence with the board's lawyer to my committee colleague, Jon Thompson, in Fredericton; he mistakenly sent it to the right telephone number but with the Montreal area code rather than the New Brunswick code and by chance it arrived on the fax machine of someone who turned the correspondence over to the *Montreal Gazette*. At that point, the board had no choice but to release the report. It also held a closed emergency meeting, the result of which was that the three faculty members involved were either dismissed or allowed to retire and both the rector and the vice-rector were forced to resign. Shortly afterwards, the board received the results of a forensic audit, which largely confirmed our findings.

What were the long-term results of our report? In due course, the university appointed a new leadership team that took on the task of tightening up its rules and procedures so as to prevent any future breaches of scholarly integrity. Alas, not every university followed suit. As one commentator noted, our report "created a brief stir in the Canadian university community but there is no indication that it did the slightest damage to the production-driven research culture that it criticized."[4] Perhaps this is not surprising given that NSERC – in a closed meeting, the results of which have never been published – subsequently exonerated at least one of the offending faculty members, whose status was then restored at Concordia. Conceivably NSERC found some flaw in our factual conclusions; possibly the agency lacked an established system of rules that would have allowed it to sanction researchers guilty of misusing funds and engaging in academic fraud. Or perhaps it felt that our report sent the research community the wrong message at a time when the promotion of entrepreneurship and private partnerships had become a dominant theme in the federal government's approach to funding research. That certainly seemed to be the view of two prominent Canadian university presidents, who issued a statement rejecting our criticism of "production-driven" research.

In the end, however, both NSERC and the university community have apparently concluded, as we did, that research must be conducted within a proper framework of rules that will ensure its integrity, and that those rules require expert, ongoing enforcement. In 2010, the Council of Canadian Academies published the report of its Expert Panel on Research Integrity, *Honesty, Accountability and Trust: Fostering Research Integrity in Canada*.[5] And in 2011 – nearly twenty years after *l'affaire Fabrikant* – NSERC and the other federal granting councils finally adopted the Tri-Agency Framework statement on *Responsible Conduct of Research*.[6]

In a sense, each of these three ventures in "useful idiocy" within the university sector ultimately produced positive results. "Ultimately" is the key word. My late friend Rod Macdonald – himself the chair of many commissions and author of many reports – made the point nicely: "Don't worry about your report being accepted by the government of the day," he told me. "Once ideas are put into circulation, if they are any good, someone someday will adopt them." This optimistic outlook sustained me through a series of rather high-profile public inquiries.

The first of these, and the one that gave me greatest pleasure, was my chairmanship of the Consultative Group on Legal Education and Research (CGREL). In 1979, the Social Sciences and Humanities Research Council (SSHRC) noted that only two legal scholars had applied for research funding that year. With the endorsement of the Canadian Association of Law Teachers and the Committee of Canadian Law Deans, in 1980 SSHRC decided to launch an inquiry into what appeared to be a serious deficit of (or disinterest in) scholarship within the legal academy. By this time I had completed my deanship, and was deeply involved in my own ambitious scholarly project, a history of the rise of the administrative state in nineteenth-century England. I had also just become a bencher of the Law Society of Upper Canada and a member of the Economic Council of Canada. Nonetheless, I eagerly accepted SSHRC's invitation to chair the consultative group that would conduct the inquiry. This, after all, would be my chance to lead the legal academy in a collective reflection on the tumultuous period of the 1960s and 1970s during which (as we all imagined) it had transformed itself.

SSHRC provided a budget for research and travel, and seconded a young and very able staff member, John McKennirey, to work with me. We soon assembled both the "Consultative Group" itself and a larger advisory committee of highly reputed members of the legal community, chaired by my mentor, Chief Justice Laskin. We pursued three strategies simultaneously: research into the quantity, quality, and content of Canadian legal education and scholarship and into the influences that may have shaped the intellectual and career aspirations of the legal professoriate; structured consultation with both producers and consumers of legal research; and intense deliberation within the consultative group itself. Each of these strategies

proved invaluable. The research studies told us a great deal about
the methodologies and subject-matter of legal scholarship and of
the academic culture from which it emerged. To mention one critical
insight: a heavy preponderance of legal scholars engaged largely or
exclusively in doctrinal research – the identification, analysis, syn-
thesis, and critique of legal rules. This explained their lack of interest
in sshrc funding, since such research required little or no financial
support other than, perhaps, the salary of a student research assistant. Moreover, the same insight also confounded the belief – widely
held by the practising bar – that Canadian scholars were interested
only in exotic (read "useless") interdisciplinary research. As a highly
regarded and reputedly progressive practitioner pronounced at one
of our consultations, "I'll read anything written by a law professor,
but I'll be damned if I'll look at an article by some silly sociologist."

Intense discussions within the Consultative Group proved especially important in the development of our report. We decided that
it was impossible to reflect on legal research and legal education
without reflecting on the nature of law and legal knowledge. One
product of that reflection was a useful, if crude, taxonomy of legal
research whose organizing vectors were, on the one hand, methodology (doctrinal analysis vs sociology, history, economics, etc.)
and on the other its intended audience (practitioners and judges vs
policy makers and law reformers).[7] This taxonomy, together with a
careful review of legal publications, enabled us to identify what was
clearly missing in legal scholarship: fundamental research intended
to deepen understanding of the causes and consequences of law and
the legal system.

We were deeply concerned about this omission. The current state
of legal knowledge, we suggested, "if it were medical, would place
us as contemporaries of Pasteur, if it related to aeronautics, as contemporaries of the Wright brothers."[8] This derogatory appraisal of
legal scholarship was paralleled by our glum conclusion that the
transformation of law faculties in the 1960s and 1970s – however
positive in other respects – had produced not a series of careful-
ly-structured alternative pathways for students with different ambitions and interests, but rather an eclectic curriculum that lacked
coherence in either pedagogy or course content. One result, amongst
others, was that nothing resembling a scholarly discipline of law had
emerged in Canada's law schools, with the long-term consequences
for legal scholarship noted above. Our report was entitled *Law and*

Learning but is sometimes referred to as the "[expletive deleted] Arthurs Report." It made extensive and, as I naturally believe, sensible recommendations to improve both legal education and legal research. It was a bestseller at the SSHRC and circulated widely abroad. However, it seems that not all of its readers enjoyed it. The practising bar initially took note of the report but thereafter ignored it;[9] doctrinal scholars in particular denounced it with considerable vitriol;[10] some law professors worked hard to discredit its analysis and recommendations and, thirty years on, continue to do so;[11] and few of our proposals have been formally adopted by law faculties.

Nonetheless, *Law and Learning* continues to have currency. It is still cited in debates over legal education and scholarship in Canada and other countries; its ideas continue to inspire the very active Canadian Law and Society Association; more and more legal scholars undertake research that addresses the fundamentals of law and the legal system, and use interdisciplinary methodologies;[12] advanced and joint-degree programs now exist in most Canadian law schools; many universities have "law and society" programs in which law is studied as one of the social sciences rather than as preparation for professional careers; several university presses now publish series entirely or primarily devoted to socio-legal scholarship; and some law schools have made serious efforts to replace their eclectic curricula with programs of study that are more carefully constructed.[13]

I wish our Consultative Group could take credit (or accept blame) for these innovative approaches to legal knowledge, education, and research. However, we can't. *Law and Learning* certainly documented and possibly legitimated those approaches, but it did not invent them. They had been developing in this country and around the world since at least the 1960s, and arguably much longer. Indeed, they represented part of a broad and long-term effort by many academic disciplines and professions to establish themselves on a new intellectual and scientific footing. That said, I am deeply concerned about the recent return of what I call "legal fundamentalism," the rejection of broad and deep intellectual inquiry as the main business of the legal academy and the corresponding assertion by an insecure profession of the preemptive claims of the supposed "basics" or "fundamentals" of legal practice.[14]

In chapter 5, I explored the return of legal fundamentalism in greater detail. Here I want simply to acknowledge what I learned too late to influence the narrative we advanced in *Law and Learning*.

No mere commission report – however carefully considered, however ineptly criticized – is likely to prevail over the powerful forces of political economy such as those that have precipitated the legal profession's current crises.[15] This creates a dilemma for "useful idiots" like myself. On the one hand, being appointed to investigate a complex problem, being provided with the resources to do so, and having an opportunity to engage with experts and stakeholders puts one in a privileged position to provide sound analysis and recommend sensible, practical solutions. But what if the "idiot" knows in advance that the analysis proffered will seem unsound to readers whose world-view (or absence of world-view) leads them to see things differently? What if the "idiot" can predict that sensible solutions are likely to appear foolish or infeasible to those to whom they are proffered because they deem themselves constrained by political or economic "realities"? Do I – the "idiot" in question – censor my analysis so that it will be palatable, even congenial, to those who commissioned the report or those who must act on it? Do I whittle down recommendations to the point where they are so innocuous that they are virtually costless, in terms of dollars or political capital?

These questions were very much on my mind as I worked my way through three major public commissions between 2004 and 2012. The first of these was a review of Part III of the Canada Labour Code – the provisions that establish minimum employment standards for the 840,000 people who then worked for federally regulated enterprises such as airlines, banks, and telecommunications companies. I was appointed in 2004 to lead the review by a minority Liberal government; part-way through my mandate, that government was replaced by the Conservatives. It would be fair to acknowledge that incoming governments usually have different priorities from their predecessors, but it is also accurate to note that the Conservatives both then and since have exhibited little or no interest in updating employment standards, let alone improving them. Worse yet, the new minister of Labour, with whom I had a cordial personal relationship, had become something of a political embarrassment to his party and therefore wielded little influence with the prime minister and his senior colleagues. Nonetheless, I organized the commission's work to maximize the chances of my report being accepted by the new government. I staffed the commission with knowledgeable individuals seconded from the Labour ministry itself; consulted extensively and intensively with my small panel of union, employer, and academic advisors; developed a strong program of research, utilizing both government resources and outside consultants; held public hearings across the country and met frequently with stakeholder organizations; and tried to ensure that my recommendations addressed issues of concern to all interested parties, as well as to the leadership of the Labour ministry.

Most of all, I tried to frame my report so that my recommendations could not be ignored. I pointed out, for example, that in response to a survey conducted by Statistics Canada at our request, federal employers had self-reported a high rate of non-compliance with the existing legislation (on average, about 25 per cent of employers failed to comply with any given provision). Moreover, although violations were clearly widespread, not one employer had been prosecuted during the preceding twenty years. I noted that the labour inspectors charged with securing compliance spent some 87 per cent of their time responding to complaints (92 per cent of which came from ex-employees) and virtually no time on educational programs or pro-active workplace audits that might have prophylactically reduced the rate of non-compliance.[16] And I discovered that in the mid-1980s, an earlier government had abandoned the practice of establishing a country-wide minimum wage and instead adopted, for federal purposes, whatever minimum prevailed in each province. This created anomalies: high-wage provinces like Alberta often had low minimums that affected very few federal-sector workers; low-wage provinces like Nova Scotia had high minimums that affected a significant proportion of the local workforce. Worse yet, the practice of "borrowing" the provincial minimum wage and applying it to federal employees did not represent an act of deliberate social or economic policy-making: it was merely convenient. I consequently recommended the re-introduction of a federal minimum wage sufficient to ensure that no federal worker would be paid so little that they could work full time for a year and still live in poverty. We did the math: raising the minimum wage to ensure that all full-time workers would be above the poverty line would have affected less than 2 per cent of the federal workforce and resulted in virtually no lost jobs.[17]

Of course, we attended to management's concerns as well, pointing out that in a modern, 24/7 globalized economy, employers needed flexibility in terms of working conditions to respond to their customers and to the inexorable demands of technology. We sketched out new legislation that (I believed) would have provided such flexibility without unduly intruding on employees' private time. We also recommended special administrative arrangements to relieve small employers of the burden of excessive paperwork. This, of course, did not placate the Canadian Federation of Independent Business, whose representatives appeared at almost all our hearings to present virtually identical submissions, and to register *faux* indignation at an ill-advised but innocuous attempt at humour by one of my academic advisors.

In due course I submitted my report, *Fairness at Work*, to the minister.[18] He organized a perfunctory press conference, thanked me in a statement that could charitably be described as terse, and hastily departed. The report then essentially disappeared from view. No front-page headlines (or back-page reports either); no questions in the House; no feverish lobbying for or against its adoption – or at least none that was visible to the naked eye. Well, perhaps I exaggerate. The *National Post* did favour me with an editorial. "Prof. Arthurs has recommended re-introduction of a national minimum wage," it said; "this is the same kind of fuzzy-headed thinking that leads people to oppose child labour." The International Labour Organization, whose Decent Work initiative I had referenced, made me the co-winner (with Nobel laureate Joseph Stiglitz) of its 2008 Decent Work Research Prize. And – as Rod Macdonald predicted – in 2015 the newly appointed labour minister in Prime Minister Justin Trudeau's Liberal government was mandated to re-visit the recommendations I had made almost ten years earlier. The ministry's review is still under way, but whatever its ultimate outcome, I am pleased to have been asked to participate.

Within a few weeks of completing my federal report, Gregory Sorbara – my former student, now Ontario's minister of finance – asked me to chair the Ontario Expert Commission on Pensions. This invitation was somewhat unexpected, as I knew nothing about pensions. Moreover, while I was to be advised by two labour-side and two management-side pension professionals, my mandate directed that I alone would write the final report.

As it turned out, I was not the only non-expert. My professional advisors included two knowledgeable pension lawyers, a labour economist, and an actuary. But as practitioners who advised individual employers and unions, they knew far more about the legal and financial aspects of individual pension plans than about the pension system writ large. Worse yet, the Ministry of Finance knew a lot less about the system than it ought to have. For example, no one in the government could accurately answer the simple question, "How many Ontarians are covered by workplace pension plans?" Statistics Canada could not answer that question; it simply republished the data it received from provincial pension regulators which, in Ontario's case, was the Financial Services Commission of Ontario. FSCO, in turn, employed student interns each summer to compile data contained in the annual returns filed by individual pension plans. Unfortunately, pursuant to an interprovincial agreement, those returns also covered numbers of active plan members and retirees who lived in other provinces and astonishingly, we discovered misplaced decimal points in the work of a few of the interns. This lack of reliable information was both startling and disappointing. On the one hand, it meant that we would have great difficulty in explaining why, as was generally assumed, diminishing numbers of workers were covered by attractive defined benefit (DB) plans. On the other, it meant that public policies affecting Ontario's growing population of retirees and large aggregations of financial capital (pension plans are second only to banks in this regard) were being constructed without a proper foundation of information.

We spent much of the next two years mining data sources so that, by the end of the commission's mandate, we could paint a fairly reliable picture of pension coverage in the province. And to its credit, the Ministry of Finance immediately set to work, in advance of our report, to assemble a team of analysts to ensure that it would have the information it needed to make policy responsibly in the future. The enhanced state of systemic knowledge generated by my team enabled me to provide a new perspective on the supposed decline of DB pensions. To everyone's surprise, it turned out that while indeed a declining percentage of the workforce enjoyed DB pensions, the actual number of recipients had remained virtually unchanged. More importantly, though many pension experts had attributed declining coverage to technical, financial, and regulatory problems, I was able to offer a much more plausible explanation. Most DB pension plans covered unionized workers, especially in manufacturing and the public service. As union density in Ontario declined from the 1970s onwards, partly as a result of a radical decline in manufacturing jobs, so too had DB coverage. Moreover, pension plans had been instituted, in the past, by employers (albeit often under pressure from unions) to provide "golden handcuffs" that would

ensure that experienced and productive workers remained loyal to
their company. However, in today's workplace, employers tended to
value flexibility over loyalty. Instead of holding on to long-serving
employees with on-the-job experience, employers are now keen to
replace them with younger, lower-paid and sometimes more tech-
savvy workers who do not expect, and will not enjoy, lengthy job
tenure. Pension plans had become not only financially burdensome,
but also counter-productive in HR terms, so far as many employers
were concerned.

These labour-market perspectives on trends in pension coverage
came as something of a surprise to most knowledgeable pension professionals and policy-makers, including some of my advisors. As I
suggested in chapter 5, experts occasionally suffer from *déformation
professionelle*: their capacity for imaginative and comprehensive analysis may be constrained by the very specialized knowledge that makes
them so valuable to their clients and so successful in their professions.
In this respect, at least, the Expert Commissioner's lack of personal
expertise in the field may have been an asset rather than a liability.

Not to overstate: I did learn a great deal from the Commission's
staff and my expert advisors, from our research consultants, and
from the many advocacy groups that presented briefs at our public hearings. By the time I sat down to write my report – *A Fine
Balance*[19] – I had a much better idea of the problems confronting
Ontario's pension regulators, providers, and professionals. My
technical recommendations for improving the Pensions Benefit Act
(largely based on recommendations from my expert advisors) were
generally conceded to be balanced and practical, and many were
indeed adopted or are on track to be. However, most of my more
ambitious recommendations for systemic and institutional reforms
have not so far been acted on.

Perhaps this was to be expected. Officials in the Ministry of
Finance had initially drafted my mandate with a view to resolving
certain technical issues. The minister, on the other hand, recognized
that the system needed to be examined from a broader perspective,
an examination it had last received a quarter-century earlier. The
compromise, which I supported, was that the technical items in
my formal mandate were book-ended by opening and concluding
language that invited (or at least permitted) my exploration of the
broader issues. That said, however the mandate was framed, it was
clear from the outset that major stakeholder groups were going to

raise whatever issues were important to them – extending the coverage of workplace pension plans, raising contribution and benefit levels under the Canada Pension Plan, and ensuring that pension legislation and regulation would keep up with world-wide developments in pension-plan design, administration, and financing. I advised the government that I would have to acknowledge any such submissions in my report but promised I would not make recommendations on any matter outside my mandate. As anticipated, many large non-mandate issues of pension policy were raised and, indeed, they often attracted more attention in the media than the issues defined in the mandate. A ministerial policy advisor began to harass me about "mandate creep," and some of the civil servants who authored the original, technical mandate did so as well. But I held to my position.

Some months after I began my work on pensions, Greg Sorbara resigned as minister of finance and was succeeded by Dwight Duncan, who was a quick study and expressed considerable sympathy for my recommendations when they ultimately appeared. At some point, the policy advisor who had been a thorn in my flesh was replaced by one more sympathetic to my approach, and with a broader vision of the whole project. And a new deputy minister of finance, Steve Orsini, had an intelligent grasp of the pension file. Why, then, despite these favourable developments, do some of my major recommendations still languish in limbo?

The answer is that they were overtaken by events. My report appeared in September 2008. A few weeks later the stock market crashed, with disastrous consequences for the solvency of many pension plans. Moreover, the general economic slowdown that had begun the previous year intensified and Ontario, like many other jurisdictions, put on hold most initiatives that required expenditures of increasingly scarce tax dollars. Finally, the future of Ontario's workplace pension plans became increasingly entangled with the outcome of a debate over whether to enhance the Canada Pension Plan or to establish a provincial counterpart. (That debate came to rest in 2016 when the federal government chose the former option.) However, sooner or later, some government will have to address the issues in my report that have so far been ignored: How to facilitate the introduction of new types of workplace pensions that respond to changing labour and financial markets? How to structure and empower a pension regulator with the capacity to intervene in timely fashion to ensure that plans do not fail? How to engage with stakeholders to ensure that review and reform of the pension system take place on an ongoing basis, rather than at intervals of two or three decades? And how to link pension policy more closely with the province's social and economic policies?

Some of these same issues resurfaced in 2010, when I was asked to review the funding of Ontario's Workplace Safety and Insurance Board (WSIB). The WSIB collects premiums from employers insured under the scheme (about 60 per cent of Ontario's workforce) and invests them in order to pay lost wages to workers suffering employment-related injuries, to pay for their rehabilitation and medical care, and to provide compensation to the families of deceased workers. The WSIB also provides financial support for the enforcement of the province's occupational health and safety laws and for programs designed to reduce the incidence of workplace accidents. Like Ontario's pension plans, the WSIB suffered significant losses in the stock market crash of 2008. However, these losses were a relatively small fraction of its huge unfunded liability – the amount by which its obligation to pay future benefits exceeded the resources presently available to do so. The magnitude of the unfunded liability – an estimated $11.7 billion – had been revealed in 2009 by a report of Ontario's auditor general. My core mandate was to investigate its causes and recommend its cure. However, as in my previous assignment, I was also asked to address a number of technical issues. These primarily concerned the methodologies used by WSIB to assess the risks associated with different types of businesses and to distribute the costs of providing benefits amongst participating employers.

Again, I played the useful idiot. I knew next to nothing about the WSIB, and even less about its financial affairs. Whatever expertise was brought to bear on the issues was provided by my tiny seconded staff, by a panel of sensible (but not in all respects expert) advisors, and by the sometimes inadequate analysis provided by WSIB's statistical and actuarial staff. I soon discovered that the existence, extent, and significance of the unfunded liability – let alone its causes and cures – were by no means agreed.

The WSIB had never been fully funded since its inception in 1914, and in the intervening years had sometimes been funded at levels much lower than those the auditor general had identified as problematic. Nonetheless, it had never failed to provide the benefits to which injured workers were entitled, no doubt because Ontario's economy and working population had been expanding, and therefore the premiums paid by employers each year kept increasing. There was no need to pay down the unfunded liability, some contended, because long-term growth would ensure that it could be sustained indefinitely. Moreover, there was serious disagreement over whether the magnitude of underfunding was much greater or considerably less than the auditor general had found. Quite understandably: after all, it is no simple task to project the value of assets and liabilities decades into the future. To do so requires the making of many assumptions about the performance of financial markets, about Ontario's economy and the growth, shrinkage, and longevity of different sectors of the insured workforce, about technology- and market-driven changes in workers' exposure to unsafe and unhealthy working conditions, about developments in medical diagnosis and treatment, and about many other matters. And to make matters worse, mistrust and hostility prevailed amongst worker and employer groups and between them and the WSIB. Each was inclined to believe that the others' estimate of the unfunded liability was driven by ulterior motives – a desire to increase premiums, for example, or a determination to reduce benefits.

My first priority was to bring an end, as best I could, to debates about whether the unfunded liability as of the end of 2009 was indeed $11.7 billion. I convened a technical consultation at which the WSIB made a full and transparent presentation of its financial analysis to an audience of labour- and employer-nominated experts(we provided funding for an actuary to represent injured workers' organizations), four neutral actuaries and economists with expertise in the field, and a consulting actuary whom I had retained as my own advisor. Ultimately, I came to the conclusion that the unfunded liability was actually about $3 billion higher than originally estimated, though some contended that it was higher yet.

With disputes over the facts more-or-less resolved, I then turned to an analysis of how the unfunded liability could have reached its present state. Information provided by public documents, by my staff, and by participants in our public hearings, led me to identify governments of all political stripes as the prime suspects. Under the relevant legislation, the government determines what benefits injured workers and their families are to receive, while the WSIB fixes the premiums employers must pay to generate sufficient funds to provide those benefits. Only if the WSIB fails to make sufficient provision can the government intervene and require it to raise premiums; governments have no power to order the WSIB to lower premiums. No power: except that they have done so time and again, sometimes clandestinely in conversations with senior WSIB officials; sometimes publicly claiming credit for the cancelation of premium rate increases as a service to employers and a boost for Ontario's economy. This conclusion did not endear me to employer organizations which lobby annually for lower premiums and which maintained that the unfunded liability was caused by lax administrative practices and overly-generous benefit payments. Nor did governments greet with enthusiasm my recommendation that they make it more difficult for themselves to do what the statute already prohibited. Nor did that recommendation placate workers' representatives who were convinced that the need to reduce the unfunded liability would be used as an excuse to lower benefits and make them even more difficult to obtain. Nor would any other recommendation easily earn their approval.

The grassroots injured-workers' movement, with which many unions and legal clinics are closely aligned, adopted a highly aggressive stance throughout my review. Its members and leaders had suffered debilitating injuries that deprived them of their livelihoods and occupational identities. Worse, as people dependent on the benefits scheme, they found themselves at the mercy of what they perceived to be an uncaring WSIB bureaucracy. And worst of all, they believed (with some justification) that their voice is not heard and their interests ignored in the formation and implementation of WSIB policies that were crucial to their well-being and dignity. They responded, for the most part, in what they took to be the only way left to them by voicing their anger at the WSIB, its policies, its management, and its staff.

Fortunately, some of the movement's leadership, and some of its allies and advisors, felt that the review provided them with an opportunity to influence the WSIB to alter its policies – especially the system of "experience rating" that, they claimed, provided incentives for employers to suppress claims. Experience rating can take many forms, but essentially it contemplates that employers with good safety records should pay lower premium rates, and those with bad records should pay higher rates. I heard from fifty or so injured workers that their employer had coerced or bribed them or otherwise arranged for their legitimate claims to be undervalued, concealed, or denied. Employers engaged in such tactics, they maintained, in order to ensure that their claims record would appear better than it was, thus earning them a more favorable rate. Earlier studies commissioned by the WSIB, academic research, and testimony from some employers all contributed to my common-sense conclusion that financial incentives designed to reduce the cost of accidents might generate illicit as well as legitimate responses. I therefore recommended that the present system of experience rating should be discontinued unless the WSIB could ensure that it was achieving its statutory objective of reducing the incidence of accidents and enhancing the return to work of injured workers. I also recommended that no new system of experience rating should be adopted until the WSIB put in place effective measures to prevent, detect, and punish illicit claims suppression.

Some elements of the employer community were outraged. Experience rating, they maintained, was no more or less than "insurance equity": those who generate higher costs for the system should, as a matter of insurance logic, pay higher premiums. In response to my observation that the present system could be legally justified only if it met specific statutory criteria, one employer-representative maintained that the statutory language had been adopted as a political ruse because it was thought to be more palatable to unions and workers than a straightforward "insurance equity" scheme. The WSIB so far has made no commitment to reform or replace the existing system. To the contrary, a recent study commissioned by the WSIB recommends adoption of a system which could conceivably embed insurance equity even more deeply in its rate-setting process, without the safeguards that I recommended. These developments have, of course, further alienated the injured workers movement.

As to the main issue facing the review, the elimination of the WSIB's unfunded liability, my main contribution was to move the debate away from zero-sum outcomes. At some level of underfunding, which I identified on the basis of advice from my consulting actuary, there is a risk that a combination of plausible events might make it impossible for the WSIB to meet its obligations. Moreover, the longer the WSIB remains at or near this tipping point, the less likely it is that benefits will be enhanced or the level of service to workers and employers improved. And finally, as the WSIB moves towards full funding, it will accumulate higher and higher financial reserves whose prudent investment will generate returns that will, in turn, permit a reduction in premium rates.

These arguments appear to have persuaded the government, the WSIB, and at least some stakeholders. Shortly after I submitted my report, the government introduced legislation mandating a twenty-year program to reduce the unfunded liability, gradually moving the WSIB away from the tipping point, though not in the precise manner that I had proposed. So far, however, the WSIB has failed to promise that it will not try to meet its mandated financial target (as I put it in my report) "on the backs of workers" by ungenerous interpretations of the statutory language that determines their entitlements, or by making claims procedures more difficult to navigate. Its failure to provide reassurance on this question, along with its inaction on the performance rating file, have left injured workers and their supporters increasingly suspicious, alarmed, and intransigent in their dealings with the WSIB.

My ambition was to use the review not just to resolve the problems that gave rise to my appointment but to persuade the WSIB and other stakeholders to deal with problems in a different way. I tried to set an example: I engaged directly and at public hearings with all interested parties; I brought their technical experts together to put to rest a controversy over the causes and extent of a critical issue, the WSIB's unfunded liability; I invited employer and worker spokespersons to separate sessions on "what I've heard" to ensure that I fully understood their positions on various issues, and then invited them to meet together to discuss my tentative conclusions in a session entitled "what I'm thinking." I also held frequent briefing sessions with WSIB's senior management, in part to dissuade it from its practice of announcing strong advocacy positions before receiving my recommendations, in part to urge it to enhance its technical capacity to deal with those recommendations when they did finally arrive, and in part to build confidence and secure buy-in for my recommendations. (For the latter reason, I also briefed the Ministry of Labour and the opposition parties both during the review and after its completion.)

To sum up, I provided a new and reliable analysis of the issues in my mandate. At least no one seriously challenged it. I then tried to build on that analytical foundation a consensus that the difficulties of policy and practice it revealed needed to be resolved, and that this might be accomplished by implementing some version of my recommendations. I never did achieve consensus – grudging acceptance might be more accurate – but the directors of the WSIB formally embraced the report and even established a "consultation secretariat" to carry on the process I had initiated. Alas, WSIB management failed to act promptly on my recommendations, or even to provide practical reassurance that it would move forward in the spirit of my report. Prospects for its implementation now seem slight.

Am I, then, a "useful idiot," or would a more accurate description omit the qualifying adjective? I will attempt an answer based on my experience as chair of half a dozen commissions (and participant in many more as a researcher, advisor, advocate, or member).

It goes without saying that commission reports should be informed by contributions from interested stakeholders, supported by careful research, and culminate in recommendations that will achieve fair and practical outcomes. Nonetheless, the formation of public policy is – ultimately, inevitably, and legitimately – a political process. Consequently, commissions and other advisory bodies can be "useful" only if they help to improve the quality of that process. In my experience they can do so in a number of ways:

- by providing a forum for a variety of views to be heard and encouraging their proponents to listen to each other
- by resolving factual controversies or finding novel solutions to difficult technical issues
- by showing that high-profile events that provoke moral panic (and prompt the appointment of commissions) are often connected to larger, systemic developments
- by brokering compromises between contending interests and ideas
- by persuading the political authorities that the public service needs new resources, structures, or mandates to do its job
- by rallying public support for worthy policies that lack a champion or discrediting those that are accorded more respect than they deserve.

That said, I acknowledge that politics must prevail in the end. Party ideologies and alliances, ministerial talents and ambitions, the business, budget, and electoral cycles, the sudden eruption of developments in other domains of public policy that preemptively claim the government's attention or drain its resources: all of these may render "useless" even the best-researched, most carefully reasoned and well-balanced commission report. Only an "idiot" could fail to understand that. On balance, I don't think I qualify, but lots of people apparently see me in that role.

Why? One obvious explanation is that I have a background as a neutral labour mediator and arbitrator, coupled with extensive hands-on practical administrative or managerial experience. Another is that though I've never concealed my sympathy for progressive causes, and often advocated for them, I've also never engaged in radical or highly partisan political activities. I'm "safe" without being totally predictable. And a third is that I'm a fast learner. As I'll explain in the next chapter, this enables me to find my way around diverse policy domains without becoming closely aligned with stakeholders whose long exposure to the field has left them knowledgeable but with fixed perspectives and entrenched positions. Whatever the reason, I have found this line of work challenging and rewarding – exactly what one needs to enliven one's retirement.

Connecting the Dots –
My Dalliance with Legal Theory

I do not hold myself out as a skilled legal practitioner, nor do I claim exhaustive technical knowledge of legislation, case law, or tradecraft in any of the legal fields in which I've been active. Nonetheless, I believe that I might have practised law with some success, had I chosen to do so. I was, after all, a pretty good articling student. As an academic, I had not only to learn the law myself but to explain it to students, and critique it on technical as well as policy grounds. As an academic administrator, I've negotiated and advocated success-fully for my faculty and my university, vetted (sometimes vetoed) the legal strategies and tactics proposed by our solicitors, and drafted university legislation. And as an arbitrator, mediator, and policy con-sultant, I've found practical solutions to often heated controversies, and managed both to rapidly understand complex legal structures and to design new and better ones.

Of course, my competence as a practitioner is neither here nor there, since I have spent my entire career *not* practising law. In the legal academy, where I have mostly earned my pay-cheques, it is one's reputation as a sophisticated theorist that counts. If I have such a reputation, I don't deserve it. I have never considered myself to be the best-read or most profound person in the room – even when I'm alone. And, as this chapter will show, I have consequently tended to be a consumer of second-hand legal and social theory rather than a primary producer.

To begin way back: legal theory counted for a lot less in the 1950s, when I was a law student, than it does today. Very likely, most of my teachers and mentors would have described themselves as "legal realists" or, as my classmate Martin Friedland suggests, Holmesians.[1]

They believed in a vague sort of way that what law actually does is as important as what law says, that law and society do not exist in isolation from each other, that law needs to adapt (and can be made to adapt) to changing social circumstances, that law is essentially an exercise in social engineering. However, they almost never discussed legal realism – or any other theory – in their classes on contracts or criminal law or the constitution, nor did they write about it much in their books or articles. Nor was legal theory featured as a free-standing subject on the curriculum of my supposedly *avant garde* law school. Indeed, there was only one opportunity for students to engage directly with theory. In our final year, we were offered the chance to take an Oxbridge-style tutorial in jurisprudence from A.B. Weston – a brilliant, madcap Australian who had joined the Royal Air Force as one of "the few" during the war, and stayed on to earn an Oxford law degree before coming to Canada. As it turned out, Weston's tutorial was not so much designed to provide students with a systematic theoretical framework for thinking about law as it was to challenge us to engage with the social and political dimensions of contemporary legal issues.

Nor did my graduate studies at Harvard provide me with much by way of theoretical perspectives on law. I enrolled in a seminar on "the state and economic life" given by the highly respected legal theorist Lon Fuller. To my regret and ire, the seminar was essentially a soapbox from which he vigorously propounded the proposition that complex, "polycentric" social problems could be managed only by dynamic systems such as markets, and not by legislation or other forms of state intervention. Fuller adhered rigidly to this approach not only in his subsequent brief career as an advisor to Richard Nixon (his former student and the 1960 Republican presidential nominee) but in his seminar as well. Our term assignment was to produce an empirical mini-study to lend support to Fuller's fulminations against state regulation. My study did just that: it showed that the market for student rental accommodation in the vicinity of Harvard Square had indeed overwhelmed the zoning and building regulations of the city of Cambridge, Massachusetts. But it did more: it showed that thanks to the triumph of the market over the state, most of us were living in housing that was shoddy, unsafe, and expensive. Fuller was not amused.

I also took a course in administrative law with Albert Sacks, a co-founder of the "legal process" school and a future Harvard dean.

Sacks's approach (like Fuller's justly famous essay on "the forms and limits of adjudication") was certainly a corrective to the implicit message of most contemporaneous law school courses that substantive legal rules are what matter rather than the institutional arrangements that bring them to life or effectively nullify them. However, Sack's implicit assumption that legal outcomes result from the operation of "neutral principles" struck me even then as naïve, as denying a basic insight of legal realism: that judges' social and political views significantly influence their decisions.

Nor did a memorable evening with an octogenarian Roscoe Pound, already enshrined in the pantheon of American legal scholarship, contribute much to my theoretical sophistication. Speaking to an audience of awe-struck graduate students, Pound described how his family's wagon was attacked by "hostile Indians" in Nebraska. "Save the rum, Roscoe," his mother cried, and, as ordered, he seized the rum supply and scooted under the wagon.[2] Alas, this encounter with a living legend left us not much wiser about "sociological jurisprudence," Pound's influential contribution that set the stage for many of the great debates in American legal theory throughout the first half of the twentieth century.

I concluded my legal education, then, as I began it: as a convinced but naïve realist, lacking anything that resembled a well-developed theory of law to frame my future scholarly endeavours. As I've mentioned, my first publication – my Harvard mini-thesis – was entitled "Tort Liability for Strikes in Canada: Some Problems of Judicial Workmanship."[3] This anodyne title was suitable for the *Canadian Bar Review*, the largely apolitical atheoretical journal in which it was published. Looking back, I can see that my concern was not so much to establish that the labour decisions of common law judges were poorly reasoned (which they certainly were). Rather it was to offer a political critique: their judgments were oblivious to, and often at odds with, Canada's public policy of encouraging the development of countervailing power in the labour market. In years to come, I became less diffident about offering a critique of law from a political or sociological perspective (but, I fear, not much more sophisticated). More significantly, in terms of my long-term theoretical development, I also proposed that labour law might be better administered through a distinctive system of expert tribunals rather than through the courts. While this notion was poorly developed in "Tort Liability," I realize now that that essay represented my first, clumsy groping towards a theoretical stance that came to be known as "legal pluralism."

My second followed soon after. In 1961, I secured a government grant to spend some time studying labour law in Denmark. This resulted in an article whose title, "Labour Lore and Labour Law,"[4] pretty much tells the story: "lore" – the practices and understandings developed by employers and unions – can and does reinforce, modify, and sometimes displace the "law" of the state. A few years later, I published a much more elaborate version of the same argument in one of my most-frequently cited works, "Developing Industrial Citizenship: A Challenge for Canada's Second Century."[5] The concept of citizenship, it turns out, had (and still has) considerable traction. As intended, it conveyed the notion that employees should enjoy in the workplace the same rights of association, expression, and due process that they are supposed to enjoy as citizens of the wider community. In addition, I wanted to conjure up the image of labour law as a semi-autonomous legal regime comprising norms, law-making institutions, and processes of dispute resolution very different from those of the general legal system.[6] Participation in the employment relation (or as I later proposed, in the labour market more generally)[7] should and did automatically entitle "worker-citizens" to the protection of that distinctive regime without their having to bargain for it.

In recent years, kindly colleagues have explained that my 1960s scholarship revealed me to be an prominent adherent of "industrial pluralism," the dominant North American industrial relations theory of the postwar era, and/or a follower of the British political economists T.H. Marshall and Harold Laski.[8] I don't dispute either characterization; in fact I am pleased to learn *ex post facto* that my work at that stage was sophisticated enough to be associated with even one theoretical tendency, never mind two or three. However, in truth, I was pretty much a theoretical illiterate. Whatever I knew about industrial pluralism came to me second-hand, via legal scholars who had obligingly incorporated its teachings into their work; moreover I was only faintly aware of Laski, and of Marshall not at all.

No less kindly commentators were closer to the mark, I think, when they recently concluded, "Arthurs does not offer a *sustained* theory of collective action or emancipation."[9] Whether or not my "industrial citizenship" theory was "sustained" (or indeed sustainable), one thing is clear: it failed to deter the powerful forces of globalization and neo-liberalism from stripping away the benefits of workplace citizenship one by one.[10] And as things turned out, labour law has become – if anything – more closely integrated into the general legal system rather than less.

Despite the failure of my "industrial citizenship" project – already obvious by the end of the 1970s – I decided to pursue the idea of semi-autonomous legal systems more generally. In part, this was an outgrowth of my interest in public law. The projection of "ordinary law" into specialized regulatory contexts was (I felt) inhibiting the effectiveness of regulatory regimes by insisting that they were accountable to the very courts whose egregious failure to protect the public interest persuaded legislators to create these new bodies in the first place. Also, as mentioned above, my interest had been piqued by a recent movement in the sociology of law that went by the name of "legal pluralism." Law-like non-state regimes, pluralists contended, subsisted everywhere – not only in pre-industrial societies (where they had long been observed by anthropologists) but also in contemporary commercial relationships, religious and ethnic communities, urban neighbourhoods, government bureaucracies, universities, and, of course, workplaces. I brought these two concerns together in the project that ultimately became a book, *"Without the Law": Administrative Justice and Legal Pluralism in Nineteenth-Century England*.[11] This was my most serious engagement with and contribution to legal theory. As I have described the historical findings of this study in chapter 4, I will focus here on its contribution to the theory of legal pluralism.

Two personal anecdotes will serve to introduce readers to that theory. The first concerns a mundane matter: how people park their cars in the Victorian cul-de-sac where I live in downtown Toronto. Since virtually no one is able to park on their own property, we all purchase municipal permits to park on the street. Since people prefer to park immediately in front of their own houses, and since the population is very stable, each person's "right" to do so has gradually come to be respected by other local residents. Unfortunately, on returning home late one evening, I found that "my" parking place was occupied, presumably by a visitor from out of the neighbourhood, so I parked in the nearest available space and went to bed – only to be awakened by the irate neighbour who "owned" the space where I had parked. His insistence that I move my car could be ignored only if I was prepared to live with the discord that my "offence" would generate, so I moved the car. My neighbour could never acquire a formal property right in his parking place by way of a common law "prescriptive easement" (unchallenged usage over a period of time), because no such easement can be claimed in a public street. However, legal pluralists would argue that he had acquired a "right to park" as an incident of life in the neighbourhood: no legislative enactment; no court adjudication; but a right that was a right in all the ways it needed to be in order to force me to move my car.

The second anecdote concerns my experience as an arbitrator in the Toronto garment industry. The industry had established its unique arbitration system in 1920, long before collective agreements became legally enforceable. My predecessor as "chair" of the system, Jacob Finkelman, had held that office for thirty years. The system was remarkably stable and remarkably efficient. Hearings were convened on very short notice; rather than calling witnesses, the parties provided an oral narrative of their case; the chair asked questions in order to reconcile the competing narratives; the hearing would last an hour or two; no legal precedents or rules of evidence were cited; no lawyers were involved in the process; the "law" governing the dispute comprised the explicit agreements and workplace customs and practices that the parties had generated through their interactions over the years; and within a day or two, the parties would receive a decision along with a practical, binding direction as to what they should do to rectify any wrongdoing. Using almost any benchmark – sensitivity to context, informality, speed, cost, the promotion of amicable relations – arbitration in the garment industry compared favourably with arbitration in other sectors, and even more so with court adjudication. However, as a reviewing court ultimately held,[12] it violated a fundamental principle of "the rule of law" because lawyers were barred from participating. Predictably, as soon as lawyers became involved pursuant to the court's ruling, the system collapsed. Legal centralism – the projection of state law into a non-state pluralistic system – had triumphed, but at considerable cost to ongoing labour-management relationships in the garment industry. (As it happened, the industry itself more or less collapsed a few years later, as a result of free trade agreements that facilitated the entry of goods made offshore with cheap labour.)

My initial contribution to the theory of legal pluralism, then, was to show that the phenomenon was ubiquitous not only in pre-industrial societies, as anthropologists had demonstrated, but in the governing structures of modernizing nineteenth-century states and in important domains of contemporary society. And not only ubiquitous, but of practical importance: indigenous, informal, "pluralistic" law – not the law of courts and lawyers – effectively governed many complex social and economic relationships. And not only ubiquitous and practical but thought-provoking as well: legal pluralism represented a challenge to lawyers' baseline assumption that law could only emanate from the state, or be authorized by, conform to, and look like state law.

Into the 1980s and beyond, my work[13] contributed to a growing literature on legal pluralism that was attracting the interest of socio-legal scholars. However, two other developments in socio-legal theory were occurring at about the same time, and they also tweaked my interest. The first was critical legal studies (CLS) – a broad but fractious movement in the American academy that generated skepticism about a number of the foundational assumptions of the legal system: that legal principles are "neutral," that legal reasoning is objective and logical, and that legal texts mean what they say. In a sense, CLS represented a much-needed updating of the crude version of legal realism that I shared with many of my academic contemporaries. However, my encounter with CLS forced me to face up to a question that somehow most legal scholars of my generation hesitated to address: Can legal institutions and processes bring about social transformation?

I started law school the year after *Brown v Board of Education*; I had just finished my second year of teaching when *Gideon v Wainwright* was decided; and I became a young-ish dean of law the year before *Roe v Wade*.[14] To my generation of Canadian legal scholars, it was very tempting to assume that if our country adopted its own version of the US Bill of Rights and appointed the right judges to our Supreme Court, we too could achieve the emancipation of racial minorities and women, we too could ensure adherence to the rule of law in the criminal justice system, we too could use law to achieve progressive changes regardless of their political popularity (or lack thereof). CLS provided me with strong reasons to resist that temptation. Ultimately, it persuaded me that law could not accomplish the emancipatory tasks assigned to it, that power relations were determined not by law but by the deep structures of political economy, and that far from ridding society of its ills, law could be, and often was, used to justify, "normalize," or obfuscate them.

However, although I greatly valued my membership in the International Network on Transformative Employment and Labor Law (INTELL) – a network of progressive scholars organized by Karl Klare, a charismatic American "crit" – I cannot say that I felt completely at home with CLS. It seemed overly influenced by its origins in American legal culture, it placed too much emphasis on legal exegesis and too little on political mobilization, and some CLS adherents seemed unduly suspicious of traditional state-centred, social democratic strategies for reforming society. On balance, though, I am hugely grateful to CLS for forcing me to think about how powerfully political economy shapes law, and how feebly influence runs in the opposite direction.

My engagement with CLS mostly took place after I re-entered academic life following the end of my presidency. Much of it also took place against the background of another major shift in socio-legal scholarship, one triggered by the rise of globalization. Traditional legal theory holds that the authority of national law depends on its promulgation by sovereign states; international law derives its authority from the willingness of states to accept conventional rules of inter-state relations, to bind themselves by treaties with other states, or to adhere to rules promulgated by international bodies they have chosen to join. Globalization poses a threat to this neat state-based understanding of law. Global business transactions, by definition, reach across state boundaries and thus operate beyond the reach of any one national legal system. However, as international law is generally concerned with inter-state relations, it fails to provide a legal framework for private business transactions. What "law," then, should govern business transactions when they sprawl across national borders? Who should resolve the inevitable disputes?

Historically, and down to the present, non-state systems of legal rules and non-state forums of dispute resolution have provided practical answers. In mediaeval Europe (as in contemporary Asia and Africa), business relationships were initially built on trading and banking networks whose members shared a common family, ethnic, regional, or religious background. As trade developed, particularly in Europe, the rules governing credit, sales, insurance, and shipping gradually coalesced into a body of generally accepted non-state law – the so-called *lex mercatoria* – administered by private tribunals established by the business community with or without the approval or acquiescence of host states. A similar development occurred in the global economy of the late twentieth century. While some international agencies acted like governments – established standards, promulgated rules, facilitated transactions, and resolved disputes – non-state private actors, especially legal and consulting firms and private arbitrators, became leading contributors to the new law of global business transactions. Thanks to them, a new *lex mercatoria* comprising a body of contractual forms and customs, rules and understandings, has developed within transnational trading and investment networks.

Of course, not all disputes occur within the business community. On the one hand, transnational corporations may feel that they are being victimized by what they perceive as protectionist measures adopted by backsliding governments in violation of their obligation to promote free trade. Many trade treaties empower private *ad hoc* trade tribunals to deal with such complaints, and even to override state laws that inhibit open access to markets. On the other, corporations frequently find themselves in conflict with indigenous peoples, labour unions, environmentalists, feminists, and other social movements. Rather than risk boycotts of their brand by consumers in the advanced economies, or sanctions imposed by governments critical of their behaviour, they agree to be bound by "soft law" norms promulgated by bodies such as the International Labour Organization (ILO), embedded in bilateral understandings with local advocacy groups or self-imposed by way of corporate codes of conduct or "best practice."

As a result of these and other developments, a body of "transnational law" has emerged that is quite different from either national or international law. Indeed, some progressive scholars claim that it is not confined to the protection of commercial interests, that it includes as well a new *lex humanitatus* – a transnational legal regime that safeguards human rights, the environment, and our common cultural heritage. But while some of its elements might be grounded in, or lead to the adoption of, formal and binding international conventions, much of this *lex humanitatus* is likely to remain forever informal and unwritten – as perhaps it must if it is to express the evolving moral expectations of the world community.

Given my extended involvement with legal pluralism, the existence of such transnational regimes as the *lex mercatoria* and the *lex humanitatus* seemed plausible enough. However, the labour lawyer in me wondered whether a *lex laboris* was also emerging: that is, a system of transnational labour law, of "labour law without the state."[15] True, labour, social, and human rights were being vigorously proclaimed in a growing number of international covenants and conventions, as integral parts of, or addenda to, trade treaties, or in the form of codes of conduct and best practice adopted by transnational corporations.[16] These transnationally generated, progressive legal norms were even said to be shaping the jurisprudence of national courts. But on the other hand, to whatever extent transnational labour law was emerging, it seemed to have made little difference to labour's ability to assert its interests in the global economy.[17] Most workers in the developed economies saw their share of GDP shrink, their economic security and standard of living deteriorate, and their influence over public policy diminish; and while the living standards of workers in many developing countries improved in an absolute sense, those workers, for the most part, continued to experience exploitation and the denial of their basic human rights.

Faced with this contradiction, I had to try to reconcile my enthusiasm for the insights offered by legal pluralism with my newly intensified convictions about the incapacity of law to transform societies. In a piece called "'Landscape and Memory,'"[18] I explored the implications of what I called "critical legal pluralism" – essentially an acknowledgement that legal pluralist regimes could no more escape the effects of unequal power than conventional state legal systems could. This sad (and perhaps belated) realization forced me to abandon my 1960s optimism about the prospects for "industrial citizenship"[19] – ironically, just as that concept was beginning to attract some attention.[20] But it also launched me on series of productive second thoughts about many other areas of my work.

As it happened, during the mid-1990s, I had become an associate of the Canadian Institute for Advanced Research (CIAR), a so-called "institute without walls." The members of its law program were all deeply committed to exploring law "in society," and to understanding law as a social science. The question was how to translate this shared commitment into a collaborative research program. The intellectual paradigm favoured by CIAR's founding president, the noted epidemiologist Fraser Mustard, was epitomized by the Whitehall study of population health.[21] That study plotted the long-term health outcomes of recruits to the British civil service on a socio-economic gradient: to oversimplify, as one descended the gradient, the outcomes deteriorated. Would a similar gradient, I wondered, describe the enjoyment of legal rights, participation in the civic and cultural life of communities, or the respect shown citizens by corporate and state bureaucracies?

Unfortunately, before our group could formulate a research strategy, Mustard retired and his successor – an economist – peremptorily cancelled the program. While the institute's new president gave financial exigency as his reason, I believe that the cancellation of our program was largely motivated by his perception that socio-legal studies lacked the scientific rigour that supposedly prevailed in his own discipline. Needless to say, I overcame my skepticism about formal state law and threatened to sue in order to force CIAR to make good on its earlier promise to fund our work for the next few years. The threat worked; we received the promised support for a limited time, but the program was terminated.

As things turned out, Mustard's "gradient" metaphor continued to influence my work. I was already committed to the proposition that the actual enjoyment of legal rights is determined not so much by the texts that express them as by the social, political, and economic power of those who claim them, and the gradient metaphor was a striking way to convey that idea.[22] More to the point, it was a powerful reminder of the need for a new science of "legal epidemiology," for a reliable approach to testing law's claims and those of its critics. However, much as I would have liked to have been a founder of that science, as I have already confessed, I remained primarily a consumer of social science research rather than a producer.

Nonetheless, as described in chapter 4, I have made at least one fairly ambitious attempt to find empirical evidence with which to test law's claims against its actual consequences. When my research assistant and I asked, "Does the Charter matter?"[23] and when we asked, "How differently, if at all, do Canadians experience their society and economy since the adoption of the Charter?" "Is there greater equality and opportunity?" "Are police and public officials more respectful of citizens' rights?" "Is our democracy more robust?" we found that evidence of positive outcomes was scant or non-existent. One might imagine that this conclusion would be of urgent interest not only to lawyers but to policy-makers and opinion-makers, scholars and social movements. Apparently, it wasn't. No one had asked these questions before we published our study in 2005; no one has done so since; and no one has revisited our study, whether to replicate it or to refute it by demonstrating its shortcomings.

I am, then, a Charter sceptic, a believer that our "real constitution" – the deep structures of our political economy – shapes the
lives of Canadians more powerfully than the Constitution Acts
themselves.[24] But I am an ambivalent rather than a gleeful sceptic. I
truly admire the efforts made by imaginative scholars and enterpris-
ing advocates to conjure up new Charter arguments. I applaud the
way open-minded judges have responded to these arguments and
made every effort to bring about progressive change – more effort,
to be honest, than I thought they would make.[25] Nonetheless, my
admiration is tempered and my applause is muted ("the sight of one
shoulder shrugging"),[26] because the evidence strongly suggests that
their efforts have been in vain. At the end of the day, I believe, progressive causes will only be advanced by social and political mobilization. At most, the Charter can help to maintain an atmosphere
in which mobilization can occur, and law more generally can help
to create the formal architecture that validates and implements the
outcomes that mobilization achieves.

So here I am at the end of my career, and of my narrative, at best
a modest contributor to legal theory. To be sure, I can see how, at
various stages in my career, I benefitted from exposure to different schools of legal thought – to a crude form of legal realism at
law school and to legal process analysis at Harvard, to the hopeful
but ill-fated 1960s project of changing the world through law by
empowering us all as "citizens," to the emerging ideas of legal pluralism in the 1970s and 1980s, to critical theory in the 1990s, and
in recent decades to a miscellany of theoretical perspectives ranging
from political economy to epidemiology to transnationalism. But to
be honest, while I was occasionally provoked or stimulated by theory, while theory sometimes provided a convenient peg on which
to hang my ideas, it was never the main driver of my scholarship.
If there has been one consistent animating principle in my work,
I suspect that it has been a rather under-theorized commitment to
small-p progressive, small-p politics, accompanied by a leavening
dose of skepticism.

Can I put a name to the theoretical approach that has shaped my
work? If pressed, I suppose I would describe myself as a connector of
dots. I have always been a fast learner, and if I'm not quite as fast as
I used to be, I still manage more quickly than most to offer a plausible account of what's connected to what, how, and why. In a sense,
this has been a detriment to my legal career. After all, the defining

characteristic of the legal mind, according to Harvard law professor Thomas Reed Powell, is that it is capable of thinking about a thing that's inextricably connected to something else without thinking of the thing to which it is connected. Lawyers, I find, are often wonderful at dealing with single instances – a business transaction, an estate plan, a lawsuit. They're so good at it, in fact, that they tend to analyze systemic issues using anecdotal rather than historical or empirical evidence. Obviously, there are exceptions, particularly amongst academic lawyers and practitioners who deal regularly with public policy issues. But given my own propensity to connect dots – to see little problems not just as examples of big problems but as an invitation to explore their underlying connections, causes, or long-term consequences – I can understand why so much of what I've been writing is regarded as outside the mainstream of legal scholarship.

Worse yet: I'm not just a connector of dots; I'm a playful connector. An observant colleague, introducing me on some public occasion, mentioned my tendency to coin catchy or humorous titles for the things I write. For example, "Extraterritoriality by Other Means" – a nod to Clauswitz's aphorism, "war is the continuation of diplomacy by other means" – was intended to signal my sardonic view that global corporations use their power aggressively to reshape whatever legal environment they encounter in their own image. Another example: "Making Bricks without Straw" takes liberties with the biblical story of Exodus in order to describe the difficulties of establishing a transnational regime of labour law.

But my best titles are not just catchy or humorous: they are, in fact, the strategy I use to connect "the dots" – the seemingly unrelated phenomena – that I am writing about. Contrary to conventional academic practice, I confess, I don't usually start work on an article by reviewing the literature or summing up the evidence. Nor when I begin to write do I first dig my theoretical foundations and then erect a narrative structure. Rather, I look for a metaphoric or allusive title that serves to link the diverse phenomena which seem to me to be related in some way that other people haven't noticed. I read rather eclectically: a daily newspaper, contemporary fiction, the *Guardian Weekly* and *New York Review of Books*, Trollope's nineteenth-century novels of English society and politics, and a good deal of biography and history (some of it sent my way by my son, a European historian). But I also read selectively: the law reports (rarely, but when necessary), academic books and articles (often generously sent to me by their authors), and a fair number of online texts (that catch my eye when they pop up on e-services to which I subscribe, like the Social Sciences Research Network). And of course, I read what others tell me I must: papers sent along by the graduate students I'm supervising, by research assistants helping me with an article, by staff on my government commissions, or by colleagues with whom I'm collaborating on academic projects (all of whom inevitably know a great deal about the many things I don't).

Thus when I sit down to write, to connect the dots, I often find myself pushing and pulling to fit my disorderly, randomly sourced ideas into a frame that will align them into something resembling a linear argument. Oddly, it is the very process of writing itself that helps me to do that. Miss Read, my high school Latin teacher, instilled in me a sense that prose should obey certain rhetorical conventions, that it should have structure, balance, rhythm. In responding to those conventions, in searching for that structure, in establishing that rhythm, I find myself addressing substantive as well as stylistic issues. Are the events described in the paragraph I've just written really commensurable? Do the ideas captured by a particular figure of speech sit uneasily side by side and might the awkwardness be eased if some of them were omitted or replaced? Is asymmetry or imbalance amongst different sections of my text a signal that I have allowed the metaphor in my title to distort my analysis? Connecting the dots in a literary sense somehow forces me to think about how to connect them substantively.

The shortcomings of this method are obvious to me. The wonder is that they don't attract more criticism from others. Perhaps readers are willing to overlook the faults in my arguments because they agree with my conclusions. Or perhaps they don't trouble to disagree because they are confident that no one will take seriously what I have to say. Or perhaps they are awed by the emperor's clothes that adorn the corpus of my scholarship – in which case I await with trepidation the outburst of a young colleague who sees how naked my arguments are but doesn't know or care that academic etiquette prevents their saying so. There may be something in this last hypothesis. Canadian legal scholars no longer use antiquated language like "with respect" or "my learned friend," but they still tend to be deferential to each other and even to the judges and commentators whose work they dissect and sometimes disparage. More importantly, they don't often engage in the intense internecine warfare that tends to erupt in other academic domains such as economics or English literature.

A case in point: my co-authored article, "Does the Charter Matter?" As I recounted earlier in this chapter, the article musters all available social statistics to support the hypothesis that the Charter of Rights and Freedoms has had far less impact on Canada's society and political economy than it has on our judges, lawyers, and scholars. In certain respects, social and economic inequality have grown rather than receded since the Charter was adopted; police and public officials have, if anything, grown more abusive rather than less so, and governments seem to conduct their day-to-day business with less regard for the rule of law and democratic practices than they did before the Charter came into force. If I had been a true believer in liberal legalism or a significant stakeholder in the Charter industry, etiquette notwithstanding I would have written a scorching rebuttal to such an article. I would have questioned its premises, attacked its methodology (which was admittedly imperfect), and deployed evidence to the contrary. I would have argued that "it's too soon to tell" whether the Charter matters, or that "things might have been even worse if there had been no Charter." At very least, I would have defended the Charter by insisting that however modest its achievements, they at least outweighed any harm it may have caused. But in the dozen or so years since the article appeared, so far as I know, it has elicited no robust critique; indeed, no critique at all. Apart from occasional fleeting references in footnotes (mostly my own), the article has virtually disappeared from view.

In academic controversies, however, one does not win by default. Silence is not taken to signal assent. I know that many, likely most, constitutional scholars do not agree with my dismissal of the great Charter project on which they have built their reputations, and in which they sincerely and optimistically believe. But why don't they say so? The answer is, I fear, that most of them do not believe in connecting dots, do not feel comfortable with systemic critique, do not want to abandon the storehouse of interesting anecdotes (also known as the Supreme Court Reports) that contains their intellectual stock in trade. No, this is not quite right: they want systems, they want order in their anecdotal storehouse, but they want to achieve order through an internal, self-referential, system of critique that does not fundamentally threaten their intellectual assumptions. However, were they to accept my analysis, were they to connect the dots as I have, they would no longer be able to defend those assumptions. They would have to abandon their worldview in which law actually "rules" and in which law sends out powerful signals that ultimately legitimate and regulate politics, markets, culture, and other modes of social ordering. And they would no longer be able to locate themselves and their fellow jurists at the centre of the legal-political universe, controlling, or at very least powerfully influencing the signals that law sends. A world without the "rule of law" would be a poorer place, they truly believe, and law not shaped by them and their Charter would be a less benign one as well.

But I am not a true believer, just a humble connector of dots.

Pessimism of the Intellect,
Optimism of the Will

I'm keenly aware that I've ended virtually every chapter in this book on a negative note. I'll recapitulate, though doing so verges on masochism.

As I considered the future of labour law, I became reluctantly convinced that the subject that was my main professional preoccupation had no future. At best, I concluded, we would have to rebuild labour law "without the state." However, this was a prospect so hopeless that I had finally to conjure up a counter-factual "law of economic subordination and resistance" in its place. Piling woe upon woe, I also had to accept that despite my six decades of tenacious advocacy there will not emerge, any time soon, a system of public law that effectively facilitates state protection of subordinate groups against abuses of private power. And once I got past my initial enthusiasm for legal pluralism as a strategy of social ordering, I had to acknowledge that non-state legal systems are just as likely as state systems to be dominated and distorted by unequal aggregations of power.

Nor do I look back on my career-long involvement with the legal academy and practising bar with much confidence that things will turn out as I once hoped. The agenda of liberal legal education and interdisciplinary scholarship my colleagues and I worked so hard to advance in the 1960s and '70s probably never did achieve the transformation of legal thought, culture, practice, and institutions that we all hoped for. Worse yet, whatever we did achieve is now under threat from the forces of legal fundamentalism, and perhaps as well from their unwitting ally, experiential learning. Nor did my service as a "useful idiot" for universities and governments fare much better. Unloved and unheeded, many of my most sensible recommendations languish in the archives or ashcans of those institutions that appointed me as a commissioner or advisor. (Here there is a glimmer of hope: change comes slowly in large organizations, so some of my recommendations may yet be adopted.)

One's successors in university administration do not hesitate to exercise their right (or perform their duty) to replace structures put in place by their predecessors. And a good thing too: this commitment to renewal has enabled some universities to survive for centuries, longer than most states and virtually all corporations. But the inevitability of institutional change may explain why universities commemorate their former presidents with brick-and-mortar memorials – a named building or, in my case, a parking-lot-turned-green-space at the heart of York's campus. This tendency to chisel in stone prompts a sobering thought. Will future generations arriving at York's "Harry W. Arthurs Common" heed the admonition inscribed on the tomb of Christopher Wren, the architect of St Paul's cathedral in London: "If you seek his monument – look around you"? Or are they more likely to recall Shelley's poem about a legendary tyrant, "My name is Ozymandias, King of Kings: / Look on my Works, ye Mighty, and despair! / Nothing beside remains."

I see myself as an architect, not a tyrant, but still ...

Here's the question I'm left with, then. How do I deal with the fact that much of my hard work has gone for naught, and that whatever apparent success I achieved in changing people's thinking, the direction of public policy, or the function of public institutions, has proved transitory? I accept, of course, that some of my efforts were misconceived or mistaken, that some things I proposed were unworkable or just plain wrong. But only by doing nothing can one be sure of avoiding error. I didn't do nothing. I was an opinionated activist. I took my chances. I know, too, that circumstances change, that what seemed like a good idea at the time may turn out to be a bad idea years or decades later, or may reasonably seem so to the people who now stand in the shoes I wore in the course of my career.

Mostly, though, over time I came to understand that while academics like me may propose, History will dispose. Neo-liberalism and illiberalism, populism and prejudice, globalization and technology, ecological disaster and even nuclear conflict – all looming large at the moment – represent imminent and existential threats to the kind of progressive law school, legal system, university, government, and society that I did my modest best to bring about. That understanding made me a pessimist, I suppose, but a pessimist of a very particular kind. As I put it in a 2009 article: "The optimists amongst us assume that human hands – our hands – shape legal education, that legal education shapes the law, and that law shapes the world. The pessimists contend that the process works in reverse, that the forces of political economy ultimately have their way with law as a system of social ordering, as a cultural phenomenon and an intellectual enterprise, and as the subject or object of study in law schools."[1] The Italian philosopher Gramsci termed this perspective "pessimism of the intellect."

However, I don't in fact feel pessimistic about my life's work. I don't arrive at the end of my narrative – and my career – in a state of dejection or disillusion. Quite the contrary: I cannot imagine that I could have led my working life much differently. When I began my career, things were not as they should be – not law schools or the legal profession, not labour law or public law. Consequently, like most conscientious young academics, I just assumed that it was my job to make them better. Perhaps I was conditioned by my family mythology, perhaps I was influenced by the spirit of the sixties, perhaps I was fulfilling my destiny as a foot-soldier in a Kuhnian revolution, or perhaps I was compulsively committing acts of ritual iconoclasm or Oedipal fury. But none of these "perhapses" seem quite right. In retrospect, it seems to me that I was simply doing what members of every generation would naturally want to do: make things better. That impulse led me to invest my energy, intelligence, and reputation in a lifelong project of reform, notwithstanding my growing comprehension of the challenges confronting any such project. Gramsci had a name for this perspective as well; he called it "optimism of the will."

Naturally, I wish that the many projects on which I embarked over my sixty or so years in academe and in public policy debates had come to more successful conclusions. Perhaps they would have done if I had done things better or differently. However, I don't plan to lose any sleep over that possibility. The roads not taken were not taken, and that's the end of it. Almost the end. The last word goes to Samuel Beckett: "Ever tried. Ever failed. No matter. Try again. Fail again. Fail better."

Notes

INTRODUCTION

1   Harry Arthurs, "Woe unto You, Judges: or How Reading Frankfurter and
    Greene 'The Labor Injunction' Ruined Me as a Labour Lawyer and Made
    Me as an Academic," *Journal of Law and Society* 29 (2001): 657; "'The
    Economy Is the Secret Police of Our Desires': York University 1985–
    1992," in *Leading the Modern University: York's Presidents on Continuity
    and Change, 1974–2014*, ed. Lorna Marsden (Toronto: University of
    Toronto Press, 2016).
2   Marie-Ange Moreau, "Cinquante ans d'analyses des mutations des
    normes du travail en Amérique du Nord: Voyage comparatiste autour de
    la pensée de Harry Arthurs," *Droit Social*, no. 3 (2015): 196; Allan
    Hutchinson et al., "Special Issue," *Osgoode Hall Law Journal* 44, no. 4
    (2006); Simon Archer, Daniel Drache, and Peer Zumbansen, *The
    Daunting Enterprise of the Law: Essays in Honour of Harry W. Arthurs*
    (Montreal and Kingston: McGill-Queen's University Press, 2017).
3   My papers have been deposited in the Clara Thomas Archives, Scott
    Library, *York University*, http://archivesfa.library.yorku.ca/fonds/
    ON00370-f0000255.htm; I have been interviewed about various aspects
    of my life and work by the Law Society of Upper Canada, Lancaster
    House publications, the Ontario Archives, and several other institutions;
    and documents relating to my maternal grandparents reside in the
    Ontario Jewish Archives.

CHAPTER ONE

1 Harry (mis-identified as "Henryk Dworkin, a Polish Jew.") is mentioned in
  Patryk Polec, *Hurrah Revolutionaries: The Polish Canadian Communist
  Movement, 1918–1948* (Montreal: McGill-Queen's University Press,
  2015), 113. See also Royal Canadian Mounted Police, Notes of the Work
  of the C.I.B. Division for the Week Ending 16 September (1920), https://
  journals.lib.unb.ca/index.php/RCMP/ article/download/ 9350/9405; Notes
  of the Work of the C.I.B. Division for the Week Ending 4th November
  (1920), https://journals.lib.unb.ca/index.php/RCMP/article/
  download/9357/9412.

2 Shmuel el Mayer Shapiro, *The Rise of the Toronto Jewish Community*
  (Toronto: Now and Then Books, 2010), http://www.billgladstone.
  ca/?p=4449; Allan Levine, *Toronto: Biography of a City* (Madeira Park,
  BC: Douglas and McIntyre, 2014).

3 Stephen A. Speisman, "DWORKIN, HENRY," in the *Dictionary of Canadian
  Biography*, vol. 15 (University of Toronto/Université Laval, 2003):
  accessed November 24, 2017, http://www.biographi.ca/en/bio/dworkin_
  henry_15E.html.

4 A plaque unveiled by the Toronto Historical Board in 2012 commemorat-
  ing the Lyceum (which has since become a Chinese restaurant) records
  Harry's contribution. I spoke at the ceremony.

5 Polec, *Hurrah Revolutionaries*, 113 n.73.

6 A brief memoir and her obituary have been reprinted online: "Toronto's
  First Jewish Nurse Writes of Early Toronto," *Bill Gladstone*, 2013, http://
  www.billgladstone.ca/?p=7453.

7 The story was related to me by Ron Daniels, then dean of the University
  of Toronto Faculty of Law, and subsequently president of Johns Hopkins
  University.

8 See Irving Abella and Harold Troper, *None Is Too Many: Canada and the
  Jews of Europe 1933–1948*, 2nd ed. (Toronto: University of Toronto Press,
  2012).

9 A plaque erected by the Toronto Historical Board c. 2010 marks the original location of the Mount Sinai Hospital and features a photo of the
  auxiliary with Dora at the centre. Not commemorated is the Dorothy
  Dworkin house, directly across the street, that housed the hospital's out-
  reach activities and was named in her honour.

10 Harry and Dora Dworkin also figured in other families' sagas. See Harry
   Rasky, *The Three Harrys* (New York: Mosaic Books, 1999) and Michael
   Mandel, *The Jewish Hour* (Toronto: Now and Then Books, 2016).

11 As of 28 September 2017, the Law Society of Upper Canada resolved to change its name (Upper Canada having ceased to exist in 1841) to the Law Society of Ontario. See Law Society of Upper Canada, "News Release: Law Society's Governing Board Votes to Change the Regulator's Name to 'Law Society of Ontario,'" LSUC, 2 November 2017, https://www.lsuc.on.ca/uploadedFiles/For_the_Public/News/News_Archive/2017/News-Name-Change-Nov-2-2017-EN.pdf.

12 I have described Laskin's influence on me in "Woe unto You, Judges: or How Reading Frankfurter and Greene, *The Labor Injunction,* Ruined Me as a Labour Lawyer and Made Me as an Academic," *Journal of Law and Society* 29 (2002): 657–66.

13 Harry Arthurs, "Labour Law – Secondary Picketing – Per Se Illegality – Public Policy," *Canadian Bar Review,* 41 (1963): 581

14 Harry Arthurs, "The Affiliation of Osgoode Hall Law School with York University," *University of Toronto Law Journal,* 17 (1967): 194.

15 I discuss this report in chapter 5.

16 Harry Arthurs, *"Without the Law": Administrative Justice and Legal Pluralism in Nineteenth-Century England* (Toronto: University of Toronto Press, 1985). I discuss this book in chapters 4 and 10.

17 Oliver Wendell Holmes, Jr, "The Path of the Law," *Harvard Law Review* 10 (1897): 457.

CHAPTER TWO

1 Friedland was a member of my law school study group; we taught together at Osgoode before he moved to the University of Toronto in 1965; he was a founding member of the Law Commission of Canada and became dean of the Faculty of Law, University of Toronto, on 1 July 1972, the same day I became dean of Osgoode Hall Law School. I strongly recommend, and have been inspired by, his excellent autobiography *My Life in Crime and Other Academic Adventures,* 2nd ed (Toronto: University of Toronto Press, 2007). And see also Martin Friedland, "Harry Arthurs: The Law Student Years," in *The Daunting Enterprise of the Law: Essays in Honour of Harry W. Arthurs,* ed. Simon Archer, Daniel Drache, and Peer Zumbansen (Montreal and Kingston: McGill-Queen's University Press, 2017).

2 See Philip Girard, *Bora Laskin: Bringing Law to Life* (Toronto: University of Toronto Press, 2005); William Kaplan, *Canadian Maverick: The Life of Ivan C. Rand* (Toronto: University of Toronto Press, 2009).

3   Harry Arthurs, "The Dependent Contractor: A Study of the Legal
     Problems of Countervailing Power," *University of Toronto Law Journal* 16
     (1965): 89.
4   Harry Arthurs, "My 'Very Idea' of Rod – and Yours," in *The Unbounded
     Level of the Mind: Rod Macdonald's Legal Imagination*, ed. Richard
     Janda, Rosalie Jukier, and Daniel Jutras (McGill-Queen's University Press,
     2015): 9–17.

CHAPTER THREE

1   I have traced the short history of academic labour law in "Labour Law as
     the Law of Economic Subordination and Resistance: A Thought
     Experiment," *Comparative Labor Law and Policy Journal* 34 (2013): 585.
     See also "Labor Law Scholarship: The Canadian Case," *Comparative
     Labor Law and Policy Journal* 23 (2002): 645.
2   "Labour Relations Law in Canadian Law Schools – Does Our Reach
     Exceed Our Grasp, or What's a Law School For?" *Canadian Legal Studies*
     1 (1964): 63.
3   I have tried to capture the dynamic of 1960s labour law and industrial
     relations scholarship in "From Theory and Research to Policy and Practice
     in Work and Employment – And Beyond?" *Industrial Relations / Relations
     Industrielles* 69 (2014): 420.
4   For a history of the US casebook group, see Lance Compa et al.,
     "Foreword," in *Labor Law in the Contemporary Workplace*, ed. Kenneth
     G. Dau-Schmidt et al. (Toronto: West Publisher, 2009).
5   "Tort Liability for Strikes in Canada: Some Problems of Judicial
     Workmanship," *Canadian Bar Review* 38 (1960): 346.
6   I recount these exciting times in greater detail in "Woe unto You, Judges,"
     657.
7   *Labour Disputes in Essential Industries* (Ottawa: Privy Council Office,
     1968).
8   "The Dependent Contractor: A Study of the Legal Problems of
     Countervailing Power," *University of Toronto Law Journal* 16 (1965): 89.
9   *Welland County General Hospital*, 16 L.A.C. 1 (1965).
10   *Russellsteel Ltd. and United Steelworkers of America*, 17 L.A.C.
     253 (1966).
11   *Port Arthur Shipbuilding Co. v. Arthurs et al.* [1966] 17 L.A.C. 109,
     quashed in [1969] S.C.R. 85.
12   *Re Men's Clothing Manufacturers Association of Ontario et al. and
     Arthurs*, 26 OR (2d) 20 (Ont.CA) (1979).

13 "The New Economy and the New Legality: Industrial Citizenship and the
    Future of Labour Arbitration," *Canadian Employment & Labour Law
    Journal* 7 (1999): 45.

14 "Developing Industrial Citizenship: A Challenge for Canada's Second
    Century," *Canadian Bar Review* 45 (1967): 786.

15 For example, "Understanding Labour Law: The Debate over
    'Industrial Pluralism,'" *Current Legal Problems* 38 (1985): 83,
    and "Labour Law without the State?" *University of Toronto Law
    Journal* 46 (1996): 1.

16 See Gregor Murray and Michel Coutu, "La citoyenneté au travail?
    Réflexions sur le milieu de travail de l'avenir / Citizenship at Work?
    Thinking the Workplace of the Future," *Industrial Relations / Relations
    Industrielles* 60 (2005): 617.

17 For an analysis of the (non)effect of the Supreme Court's decisions, see
    "Of Skeptics and Idealists: Bernie and Me and the Right to Strike,"
    Canadian Labour & Employment Law Journal 19 (2015–16): 327.

18 "Understanding Labour Law," note 16.

19 "Globalization of the Mind: Canadian Elites and the Restructuring of
    Legal Fields," *Canadian Journal of Law and Society* 12 (1998): 219.

20 "Developing Industrial Citizenship."

21 "Post-modern Times: Charlie Chaplin and the New World of Work," in
    HRDC/OECD *Conference on Changing Workplace Strategies* (Ottawa: HRDC
    Canada, 1996); *The New Economy and the Demise of Industrial
    Citizenship* (Kingston: IRC Press, 1997); "Labour Law and Industrial
    Relations in the Global Economy," *Industrial Law Journal (S Africa)* 18
    (1997): 571.

22 "Labour Law without the State?" 1.

23 "'Landscape and Memory': Labour Law, Legal Pluralism and
    Globalization," in *Advancing Theory in Labour Law in a Global Context*,
    ed. T. Wilthagen (Amsterdam: North Holland Press, 1997), 21.

24 "Who's Afraid of Globalization? The Transformation of Canadian Labour
    Law," in *Globalization and the Future of Labour Law*, ed. J. Craig and M.
    Lynk (Cambridge: Cambridge University Press, 2005), 51; "The False
    Promise of the Sharing Economy," in *Law and the "Sharing Economy":
    Regulating Online Market Platforms*, ed. D. McKee, F. Makela, and T.
    Scassa (Ottawa: University of Ottawa Press, 2017).

25 "Labour Law after Labour," in *The Idea of Labour Law*, ed. Guy Davidov
    and Brian Langille (Oxford: Oxford University Press, 2010), 13.

26 "Reinventing Labor Law for the Global Economy," *Berkeley Journal of
    Employment and Labor Law* 22 (2001): 271.

27   "Reconciling Differences Differently: Reflections on Labor Law and
      Worker Voice after Collective Bargaining," *Comparative Labour Law and
      Policy Journal* 28 (2007): 155.
28   "Private Ordering and Workers' Rights in the Global Economy: Corporate
      Codes of Conduct as a Regime of Labour Market Regulation," in *Labour
      Law in an Era of Globalization: Transformative Practices and Possibilities*,
      ed. J. Conaghan, K. Klare, and M. Fischl (Oxford: Oxford University
      Press, 2001), 471; "Corporate Self-regulation: Political Economy, State
      Regulation and Reflexive Labour Law," in *Regulating Labour in the Wake
      of Globalisation*, ed. C. Estlund and B. Bercusson (Oxford: Hart
      Publishing, 2007), 19; Harry Arthurs and Claire Mummé, "From
      Governance to Political Economy: Insights from a Study of Relations
      between Corporations and Workers," *Osgoode Hall Law Journal* 45
      (2007): 439; "The Pachyderm and the Predator: Two Fables about the
      Social Regulation of the Global Firm," in *The Regulation of Work and
      Employment in Global Firms*, ed. Gregor Murray and Gilles Trudeau
      (Oxford: Routledge, 2014).
29   "The Hollowing Out of Corporate Canada: Implications for
      Transnational Labor Law, Policy and Practice," *Buffalo Law Review* 57
      (2009): 781.
30   "Labour and the 'Real' Constitution," *Cahiers du droit* 48 (2007): 43;
      "The Constitutionalization of Employment Relations: Multiple
      Models, Pernicious Problems," *Social and Legal Studies* 19 (2010): 403;
      "Constitutionalizing the Right of Workers to Organize, Bargain and
      Strike: The Sight of One Shoulder Shrugging," *Canadian Labour &
      Employment Law Journal* 15 (2010): 273; "Of Skeptics and Idealists,"
      327.
31   "Labour Law as the Law of Economic Subordination and Resistance: A
      Thought Experiment," *Comparative Labor Law and Policy Journal* 34
      (2013): 585.
32   "From Theory and Research to Policy and Practice in Work and
      Employment – And Beyond?"

CHAPTER FOUR

1   Economic Council of Canada, *Reforming Regulation* (Ottawa: Minister of
     Supply and Services Canada, 1981).
2   *Royal Commission Inquiry into Civil Rights* (Toronto: Queen's Printer,
     1968), https://archive.org/details/royalcommissionio1onta.

3 I canvassed these ideas in "Rethinking Administrative Law: A Slightly Dicey Business," *Osgoode Hall Law Journal* 17 (1979): 1 and "Jonah and the Whale: The Appearance, Disappearance and Reappearance of Administrative Law," *University of Toronto Law Journal* 30 (1980): 225.

4 "Protection against Judicial Review," *Revue du Barreau* 43: 277–90, reprinted in Canadian Institute for the Administration of Justice, *Judicial Review of Administrative Rulings* (Montreal: Editions Y. Blais, 1983).

5 *Port Arthur Shipbuilding Co.,* [1966] 17 L.A.C. 109 and *Men's Clothing Industry,* 26 OR (2d) 20 (Ontario, CA) (1979) – both discussed in chapter 3.

6 *"Without the Law": Administrative Justice and Legal Pluralism in Nineteenth-Century England* (Toronto: University of Toronto Press, 1985).

7 *Czarnikow v. Roth, Schmidt,* [1922] 2 K.B. 478, 488 (per Scrutton L.J.).

8 *Crevier* v Québec *(AG),* [1981] 2 S.C.R. 220.

9 *C.U.P.E. v. N.B. Liquor Corporation,* [1979] 2 S.C.R. 227. Apparently my arguments persuaded at least a few judges to intervene less aggressively in administrative proceedings; see the judgment of Wilson J. in *National Corn Growers Association v Canada,* [1990] 2 S.C.R. 1324.

10 "Mechanical Arts and Merchandise: Canadian Public Administration in the New Economy," *McGill Law Journal* 42 (1997): 29; "Governance after the Washington Consensus: The Public Domain, the State and the Microphysics of Power," *Man and Development* 29 (2002): 85; "Governing the Canadian State: The Constitution in an Era of Globalization, Neo-Liberalism, Populism, Decentralization and Judicial Activism," *Constitutional Forum* 13 (2003): 60; "The Administrative State Goes to Market – and Cries Wee, Wee, Wee All the Way Home," *University of Toronto Law Journal* 55 (2005): 797.

11 "Globalization of the Mind: Canadian Elites and the Restructuring of Legal Fields," *Canadian Journal of Law and Society* 12 (1998): 219.

12 "TINA x 2: Constitutionalizing Neo-conservatism and Regional Economic Integration," in *Room to Manoeuvre? Globalization and Policy Convergence,* ed. T.J. Courchene (Montreal and Kingston: McGill-Queen's University Press, 1999), 17.

13 "The Hollowing Out of Corporate Canada?" in *Globalizing Institutions: Case Studies in Social Regulation and Innovation,* ed. J. Jenson and B. Santos (London: Ashgate Press, 2001), 29.

14 "The Hollowing Out of Corporate Canada: Implications for Transnational Labor Law, Policy and Practice," *Buffalo Law Review* 57 (2009): 781.

15 "Governing the Canadian State," 60; "Governance after the Washington Consensus," 85.

16   "Mechanical Arts and Merchandise," 29; "The Administrative State Goes to Market – and Cries Wee, Wee, Wee All the Way Home," 797.

17   The phrase was used by Alexander Hamilton in *Federalist Papers No. 78*. The courts, he noted, "have no influence over either the sword or the purse." avalon.law.yale.edu/18ᵗʰ_century/fed78.asp. It was adopted with ironic overtones as the title of Alexander M. Bickel's critical history of the US Supreme Court, *The Least Dangerous Branch: The Supreme Court at the Bar of Politics* (New Haven: Yale University Press, 1962).

18   "Hate Propaganda – an Argument against Attempts to Stop It by Legislation," *Chitty's Law Journal* 18 (1970): 1.

19   "Civil Liberties – Public School – Segregation of Negro Students," *Canadian Bar Review* 41 (1963): 453.

20   "'The Right to Golf": Reflections on the Future of Workers, Unions and the Rest of Us under the Charter," *Queen's Law Journal* 13, 2 (1989): 217.

21   "Labour and the 'Real' Constitution," *Cahiers du droit* 48 (2007): 43–64; "Constitutionalizing the Right of Workers to Organize, Bargain and Strike: The Sight of One Shoulder Shrugging," *Canadian Labour & Employment Law Journal* 15 (2010): 273.

22   See e.g. *Consolidated Fastfrate Inc. v.* Western Canada Council of Teamsters, [2009] 3 S.C.R. 407.

23   "Vox Populi: Populism, the Legislative Process and the Canadian Constitution," in *The Least Examined Branch: The Role of Legislatures in the Constitutional State*, ed. R. Baumann and T. Kahane (New York: Cambridge University Press, 2006), 155.

24   Harry Arthurs and Brent Arnold, "Does the Charter Matter?" *Review of Constitutional Studies* 11 (2005): 37.

25   "Of Skeptics and Idealists: Bernie and Me and the Right to Strike," *Canadian Labour & Employment Law Journal* 19 (2015–16): 327.

26   "Labour and the 'Real' Constitution," *Cahiers du droit* 48 (2007): 43.

27   "Constitutional Courage" *McGill Law Journal* 49 (2003): 3; "Vox Populi," 155; "Constitutionalism – An Idea Whose Time Has Come ... and Gone?" *Amicus Curiae* 75, 3 (2008): 3.

28   Pierre Elliott Trudeau, "Economic Rights," *McGill Law Journal* 8 (1961): 122.

CHAPTER FIVE

1   Harry Arthurs, "The Affiliation of Osgoode Hall Law School with York University," *University of Toronto Law Journal* 17 (1967): 194.

2 I have written about Le Dain elsewhere. See "A Locomotive of a Man: Gerald Le Dain in Memoriam," *Osgoode Hall Law Journal* 45 (2008): 660 and "The Tree of Knowledge / The Axe of Power: Gerald Le Dain and the Transformation of Canadian Legal Education," in *Tracings of Gerald Le Dain's Life in the Law*, ed. G.B. Baker and Richard Janda (Montreal: McGill-Queen's University Press, 2018).

3 H. Arthurs, L. Taman, and J. Willms, "The Toronto Legal Profession: An Exploratory Survey," *University of Toronto Law Journal* 21 (1971): 498–528.

4 "The Study of the Legal Profession in the Law School," *Osgoode Hall Law Journal* 8 (1970): 183; "Authority, Accountability, and Democracy in the Government of the Ontario Legal Profession," *Canadian Bar Review* 49 (1971): 1; "Towards a Humane Professionalism: Lawyering and the Convivial Society," in *Law, Growth and Technology*, ed. D. Weisstub (CIDOC, 1972); "The Professions and Competition Policy," in *Canadian Competition Policy for the 1970's* (Kingston: Queen's University Industrial Relations Centre, 1972), 50; "Progress and Professionalism: The Canadian Legal Profession in Transition," in *Law and Social Change*, ed. J. Ziegel (1972), 1; H. Arthurs and P. Verge, "The Future of Legal Services / Services juridiques de l'avenir," *Canadian Bar Review* 51 (1973): 15–31; "Clients, Counsel & Community," *Osgoode Hall Law Journal* 11 (1973): 437; "Barristers and Barricades: Prospects for the Lawyer as a Reformer," *University of Western Ontario Law Review* 15 (1976): 59; "Paradoxes of Canadian Legal Education," *Dalhousie Law Review* 3 (1977): 639.

5 H. Arthurs, R. Weisman, and F. Zemans, "Canadian Lawyers: A Peculiar Profession," in *Lawyers in Society: The Common Law World*, ed. R. Abel and P. Lewis (Berkeley: University of California Press, 1988), 123–85. I also began work on an economic and sociological study of the profession in collaboration with David Stager, an economist. However, I had to abandon it part-way through because of the pressure of presidential responsibilities. See *The Canadian Legal Profession* (Toronto: University of Toronto Press, 1990).

6 H. Arthurs and R. Kreklewich, "Law, Legal Institutions, and the Legal Profession in the New Economy," *Osgoode Hall Law Journal* 34 (1996): 1; "Lawyering in Canada in the 21st Century," *Windsor Yearbook of Access to Justice* 15 (1996): 202; "Poor Canadian Legal Education: So Near to Wall Street, So Far from God," *Osgoode Hall Law Journal* 38 (2001): 381; "The World Turned Upside Down: Are Changes in Political Economy and Legal Practice Transforming Legal Education and

Scholarship? Or Vice Versa?" *International Journal of the Legal Profession* 8 (2001): 11; "The State We're In: Legal Education in Canada's New Political Economy," *Windsor Yearbook of Access to Justice* 20 (2001): 35.

7 "The Hollowing Out of Corporate Canada?" in *Globalizing Institutions: Case Studies in Social Regulation and Innovation*, ed. J. Jenson and B. Santos (London: Ashgate Press, 2001), 29.

8 "'Valour rather than Prudence': Hard Times and Hard Choices for Canada's Legal Academy," *Saskatchewan Law Review* 76 (2013): 73; "The Future of Legal Education: Three Visions and a Prediction," *Alberta Law Review* 51 (2014): 705; "The Tree of Knowledge / The Axe of Power."

9 Lakehead University in Thunder Bay, Ontario, won approval for a truncated program on the grounds that it was preparing its graduates to serve small Northern, aboriginal, and rural communities, all of which experience a serious deficit of lawyers. As of the time of writing, Ryerson University in Toronto – with a similar truncated, practice-based program – has been accredited by the Law Society and is awaiting government funding approval.

10 The Supreme Court of Canada has recently rejected the establishment of a law school at Trinity Western University in British Columbia on the basis of objections by the Law Society of British Columbia to the university's "community covenant," which requires students and faculty to adhere to its evangelical principles. See *Law Society of British Columbia v Trinity Western University*, 2018 S.C.C. 32.

11 "Will the Law Society of Alberta Celebrate Its Bicentenary?" *Alberta Law Review* 45 (2008): 15.

12 "'Valour rather than Prudence,'" 73; "The Future of Legal Education," 705.

CHAPTER SIX

1 "Globalization of the Mind: Canadian Elites and the Restructuring of Legal Fields," *Canadian Journal of Law and Society* 12 (1998): 219.

2 "TINA x 2: Constitutionalizing Neo-conservatism and Regional Economic Integration," in *Room to Manoeuvre? Globalization and Policy Convergence*, ed. T.J. Courchene (Montreal and Kingston: McGill-Queen's University Press, 1999), 17.

3 "The Re-constitution of the Public Domain," in *The Market or the Public Domain: Global Governance and the Asymmetry of Power*, ed. D. Drache and R. Higgott (London: Routledge, 2001), 85; "Governance after the Washington Consensus: The Public Domain, the State and the Microphysics of Power," *Man and Development* 29 (2002): 85;

"Governing the Canadian State: The Constitution in an Era of Globalization, Neo-Liberalism, Populism, Decentralization and Judicial Activism," *Constitutional Forum* 13 (2003): 60.

4 "Labour Law without the State?" *University of Toronto Law Journal* 46 (1996): 1; "Labour Law and Industrial Relations in the Global Economy," *Industrial Law Journal* 18 (1997): 571; "A Collective Labour Law for the Global Economy?" in *Labour Law and Industrial Relations at the Turn of the Century: Liber Amicorum in Honour of Roger Blanpain*, ed. C. Engels and M. Weiss (The Hague/London/ Boston: Kluwer, 1998), 143; "Reinventing Labor Law for the Global Economy," *Berkeley Journal of Employment and Labor Law* 22 (2001): 271.

5 "The Role of Global Law Firms in Constructing or Obstructing a Transnational Regime of Labour Law," in *Rules and Networks: The Legal Culture of Global Business Transactions*, ed. R. Appelbaum, W. Felstiner, and V. Gessner (Oxford: Hart Publishing, 2001), 273.

6 "Private Ordering and Workers' Rights in the Global Economy: Corporate Codes of Conduct as a Regime of Labour Market Regulation," in *Labour Law in an Era of Globalization: Transformative Practices and Possibilities*, ed. J. Conaghan, K. Klare, and M. Fischl (Oxford: Oxford University Press, 2001), 471; "Corporate Codes of Conduct: Profit, Power and Law in the Global Economy," in *Ethics Codes, Corporations and the Challenges of Globalization*, ed. W. Cragg (Cheltenham, UK: Edward Elgar Press, 2005), 51; "Corporate Self-regulation: Political Economy, State Regulation and Reflexive Labour Law," in *Regulating Labour in the Wake of Globalisation*, ed. C. Estlund and B. Bercusson (Oxford: Hart Publishing, 2007), 19.

7 "Making Bricks without Straw: The Creation of a Transnational Labour Regime," in *Critical Legal Perspectives on Global Governance: Liber Amicorum David M. Trubek*, ed. Claire Kirkpatrick, Joanne Scott, and Gráinne de Búrca (Oxford: Hart Publishing, 2014), 129.

8 "'Landscape and Memory': Labour Law, Legal Pluralism and Globalization," in *Advancing Theory in Labour Law in a Global Context*, ed. T. Wilthagen (Amsterdam: North Holland Press, 1997), 21; "Globalization and Its Discontents," in *The Vancouver Institute: An Experiment in Public Education*, ed. P. Nemetz (Vancouver: JBA Press, 1998), 132; "A Collective Labour Law for the Global Economy?" 143; "A Global Code of Ethics for the Transnational Legal Field?" *Legal Ethics* 2 (1999): 21.

9 "Extraterritoriality by Other Means: How Labor Law Sneaks across Borders, Conquers Minds and Controls Workplaces Abroad," *Stanford Law & Policy Review* 21 (2010): 527.

10 "Labour Law and Transnational Law: The Fate of Legal Fields / The Trajectory of Legal Scholarship," in *The London Lectures on Transnational Law and Global Governance: Keynote Lectures from the Inaugural Transnational Law Summer Institute, King's College London,* ed. Prahba Kotiswaran and Peer Zumbansen (Cambridge: Cambridge University Press, 2017).

11 *Labour Disputes in Essential Industries* (Ottawa: Privy Council Office, 1968).

12 "I Am Curious (Red and White): A Canadian Reaction to Sweden's New Industrial Ideology," in *Conference on the Swedish Industrial Democracy Act, Institute of Industrial Relations* (Los Angeles: University of California, 1975), http://digitalassets.lib.berkeley.edu/irle/ucb/text/irla0014.pdf.

13 B.A. Aaron and K.V.W. Stone, ed. *Rethinking Comparative Labor Law: Bridging the Past and the Future* (Lake Mary, Florida: Vandeplas Publishing, 2007).

14 "Compared to What? Reflections on the Future of Comparative Labor Law," *Comparative Labor Law & Policy Journal* 28 (2007): 60.

15 "Where Have You Gone, John R. Commons, Now That We Need You So? (Review of Daniel T. Rodgers, 'Atlantic Crossings: Social Politics in a Progressive Age')," *Comparative Labor Law and Policy Journal* 21 (2001): 373.

16 "Cross-national Legal Learning: The Uses of Comparative Labour Knowledge, Law and Policy," in *Re-thinking Employment Regulation: Beyond the Standard Contract of Employment,* ed. Katherine Stone and Harry Arthurs (New York: Russell Sage Foundation, 2013), 353.

CHAPTER SEVEN

1 The building committee was ably chaired by Professor Dennis Hefferon.

2 I have provided an account of Le Dain's deanship in "The Tree of Knowledge / The Axe of Power: Gerald Le Dain and the Transformation of Canadian Legal Education," in *Tracings of Gerald Le Dain's Life in the Law,* ed. G.B. Baker and Richard Janda (Montreal: McGill-Queen's University Press, 2018).

3 My own role in these crises has been described in J.T. Saywell, *Someone to Teach Them: York and the Great University Explosion 1960–1973* (Toronto: University of Toronto Press, 2008), 13–14.

4 When British Columbia elected its first-ever NDP government in 1972 –
   weeks after I became dean – three Osgoode faculty members were
   appointed to senior positions in that province's public service.

5 "The Political Economy of Canadian Legal Education," *Journal of Law &
   Society* 25 (1998): 14.

6 Michiel Horn, *York University: The Way Must Be Tried* (Montreal and
   Kingston: McGill-Queen's University Press, 2009); Harry Arthurs, "'The
   Economy Is the Secret Police of Our Desires': York University 1985–1992,"
   in *Leading the Modern University: York's Presidents on Continuity and
   Change, 1974–2014*, ed. Lorna Marsden (Toronto: University of Toronto
   Press, 2016).

7 *The Ivory Tower and the Boardroom: The University as an Organizational
   Laboratory* (Toronto: Empire Club of Toronto, 1990), http://speeches.
   empireclub.org/61221/data?n=5.

8 Harry Arthurs and Brent Arnold, "Does the Charter Matter?" *Review of
   Constitutional Studies* 11 (2005): 37.

9 "Drowning by Numbers: The Humanities and University Decision-
   Making," in *The Humanities and the Future of the University*, ed. J.
   Murray and M. Pufahl (Windsor, Ontario: Humanities Research Group,
   University of Windsor, 1997), 39.

CHAPTER EIGHT

1 Julian Webb, "The 'Ambitious Modesty' of Harry Arthurs' Humane
   Professionalism," *Osgoode Hall Law Journal* 44 (2006): 119.

2 For an account of Canadian labour law pedagogy in the 1960s, and of the
   challenges I encountered as a young teacher, see "Labour Relations Law in
   Canadian Law Schools – Does Our Reach Exceed Our Grasp, or What's a
   Law School For?" *Canadian Legal Studies* 1 (1964): 63.

3 *Cooper v Wandsworth Board of Works*, 143 ER 414 (1863).

4 "Law and Learning in an Age of Globalization," *German Law Journal* 10
   (2014): 629, http://ssrn.com/abstract=1478722.

5 Lorne Sossin, "Experience the Future of Legal Education," *Alberta Law
   Review* 51 (2014): 854.

6 Fred Zemans, "The Dream Is Still Alive," *Osgoode Hall Law Journal* 35
   (1997): 513.

7 See *Law and Learning: Report of the Consultative Committee on
   Research and Education in Law* (Ottawa: Minister of Supply and Services,
   1983), 51 ff, and recommendation 5 at 155.

8   See e.g. "Prometheus Unbound: Law in the University," *University of New Brunswick Law Journal* 38 (1989): 75; "Law and Learning in an Age of Globalization," *German Law Journal* 10 (2014): 629; "'Valour Rather than Prudence': Hard Times and Hard Choices for Canada's Legal Academy," *Saskatchewan Law Review* 76 (2013): 73; "The Future of Legal Education: Three Visions and a Prediction," *Alberta Law Review* 51 (2014): 705.

9   Some of these testimonials are found in Richard Janda, Rosalie Jukier, and Daniel Jutras, ed. *The Unbounded Level of the Mind: Rod Macdonald's Legal Imagination* (Montreal and Kingston: McGill-Queen's University Press, 2015).

CHAPTER NINE

1   See Morris Wolfe, OCA *1967–1972: Five Turbulent Years* (Toronto: Grubstreet Books, 2002).

2   Harry Arthurs and Joyce Lorimer, *The External Review of the Administration of Trent University: Final Report* (Peterborough, ON: Trent University, 1997).

3   Independent Committee of Inquiry into Academic and Scientific Integrity, *Integrity in Scholarship: A Report to Concordia University* (Montreal: Concordia University, 1994). For extended accounts of the murders and their sequel, see Morris Wolfe, "Dr. Fabrikant's Solution," in *Saturday Night* (July/August 1994), http://www.grubstreetbooks.ca/essays/fabrikant12.html and Wilfred Cude, *The PhD Trap Revisited* (Toronto: Dundurn, 2000), 113 ff.

4   Michael Skolnik, "Does Counting Publications Provide Any Useful Information about Academic Performance?" *Teacher Education Quarterly* (Spring 2000): 20.

5   Expert Panel on Research Integrity, *Honesty, Accountability and Trust: Fostering Research Integrity in Canada* (Ottawa: Council of Canadian Academies, 2010), http://www.scienceadvice.ca/uploads/eng/ assessments%20and%20publications%20and%20news%20releases/ research%20integrity/ri_report.pdf.

6   Canadian Institutes of Health Research, *Tri-Agency Framework: Responsible Conduct of Research* (Ottawa: Secretariat on Responsible Conduct of Research, 2016), www.rcr.ethics.gc.ca/eng/policy-politique/ framework-cadre/#21.

7   *Law and Learning: Report of the Consultative Committee on Research and Education in Law* (Ottawa: Minister of Supply and Services, 1983), 67.

8   *Law and Learning*, 70.

9   The Federation of Law Societies of Canada sponsored a conference at
     which *Law and Learning* was extensively discussed. See R.J. Matas and
     D.J. McCawley, ed. *Legal Education in Canada: Reports and Background
     Papers of a National Conference on Legal Education* (Winnipeg: 23–26
     October 1985).

10   See e.g. Mark Weinberg, "On the Relationship of *Law and Learning* to
     Law and Learning," *McGill Law Journal* 29 (1983): 155, and the con-
     temporary account of a young law professor of the reception of the
     report at her law school, Constance Backhouse, "Revisiting the Arthurs
     Report Twenty Years Later," *Canadian Journal of Law and Society* 18
     (2003): 33.

11   A former law teacher, now a senior practitioner, responded to a recent
     article of mine on legal education: "the original Arthurs' Report did huge
     damage to legal education – for me, personally, I was told that, as a
     scholar focused on mere doctrine, I had no place in a law school; I should
     have been 'doing' law and … economics, philosophy, sociology, dentistry,
     basket-weaving or something else, anything but law." See "Thursday
     Thinkpiece: Arthurs on Legal Education," *Slaw* (30 May 2013), http://
     www.slaw.ca/ 2013/05/30/Thursday-thinkpiece-arthurs-on-legal-
     fundamentalism/comment-page-1/.

12   Harry Arthurs and Annie Bunting, "Socio-legal Scholarship in Canada: A
     Review of the Field," *Journal of Law and Society* 41 (2014): 487.

13   "Madly Off in One Direction: McGill's New Integrated, Poly-Jural, Trans-
     systemic Law Program," *McGill Law Journal* 50 (2005): 706.

14   I have elaborated on these concerns in a series of recent articles: "'Valour
     Rather than Prudence': Hard Times and Hard Choices for Canada's Legal
     Academy," *Saskatchewan Law Review* 76 (2013): 73; "The Future of
     Legal Education: Three Visions and a Prediction," *Alberta Law Review* 51
     (2014): 705; "The Tree of Knowledge / The Axe of Power: Gerald Le Dain
     and the Transformation of Canadian Legal Education," in *Tracings of
     Gerald Le Dain's Life in the Law*, ed. G.B. Baker and Richard Janda
     (Montreal: McGill-Queen's University Press, 2018).

15   I wish I had been more cognizant of this fact when we were writing our
     report. See Harry Arthurs, "The Political Economy of Canadian Legal
     Education," *Journal of Law and Society* 25 (1998): 14.

16   *Fairness at Work: Federal Labour Standards for the 21st Century*
     (Gatineau: Government of Canada, 2006), c 9.

17   *Fairness at Work,* 245 ff.

18   *Fairness at Work,* c 9.

19   *A Fine Balance: Safe Pensions / Affordable Plans / Fair Rules* (Toronto:
     Queen's Printer for Ontario, 2008).

CHAPTER TEN

1   Martin Friedland, "Harry Arthurs: The Law Student Years," in *The
     Daunting Enterprise of the Law: Essays in Honour of Harry W. Arthurs*,
     ed. Simon Archer, Daniel Drache, and Peer Zumbansen (Montreal and
     Kingston: McGill-Queen's University Press, 2017), 333.

2   Does my memory play tricks or did Pound's? As numerous biographies
     confirm, his family emigrated from New York to Nebraska before he was
     born, and he grew up in the small city of Lincoln, Nebraska, where his
     father was a judge. When and where might such an attack have occurred?

3   "Tort Liability for Strikes in Canada: Some Problems of Judicial
     Workmanship," *Canadian Bar Review* 38 (1960): 346.

4   "Labour Lore and Labour Law: A North American View of the Danish
     Experience," *International and Comparative Law Quarterly* 12, 1 (1963):
     247.

5   "Developing Industrial Citizenship: A Challenge for Canada's Second
     Century," *Canadian Bar Review* 45 (1967): 786.

6   "Understanding Labour Law: The Debate Over 'Industrial Pluralism,'"
     Current Legal Problems 38 (1985): 83.

7   "Charting the Boundaries of Labour Law: Innis Christie and the Search
     for an Integrated Law of Labour Market Regulation," *Dalhousie Law
     Journal* 34 (2011): 1.

8   Eric Tucker, "A Tale of Two Harrys: The Life and Demise of Industrial
     Pluralism in Canada"; Gregor Murray, "The Once and Future Industrial
     Citizen" in *The Daunting Enterprise of the Law*.

9   Simon Archer, Daniel Drache, and Peer Zumbansen, "Introduction," in
     The Daunting Enterprise, 12

10   Harry Arthurs, *The New Economy and the Demise of Industrial
     Citizenship* (Kingston, ON: IRC Press, 1997), 1.

11   *"Without the Law": Administrative Justice and Legal Pluralism in
     Nineteenth Century England* (Toronto: University of Toronto Press, 1985).

12   *Re Men's Clothing Manufacturers Association of Ontario and Toronto
     Joint Board, Amalgamated Clothing and Textile Workers' Union*, 22 LAC
     (2d) 328 (Ont. Div. Ct.) (1979).

13   "Rethinking Administrative Law: A Slightly Dicey Business," *Osgoode
     Hall Law Journal* 17 (1979): 1; "Alternatives to the Formal Justice System:

Reminiscing about the Future," in *Conference Proceedings, The Cost of Justice* (Toronto: CIAJ/Carswell, 1980), 1; "Special Courts, Special Law: Legal Pluralism in Nineteenth-Century England," in *Law, Economy & Society: Essays in the History of English Law 1750–1914*, ed. G. Rubin and D. Sugarman (Abingdon, UK: Professional Books, 1984), 380; "'Without the Law': Courts of Local and Special Jurisdiction in Nineteenth-Century England," in *Customs, Courts and Counsel, Proceedings, Sixth British Legal History Conference*, ed. A. Kiralfy, M. Slatter, and R. Virgoe (London: Frank Cass, 1984), 130; "Understanding Labour Law: The Debate over 'Industrial Pluralism,'" *Current Legal Problems* 38 (1985): 83; "Labour Law without the State?" *University of Toronto Law Journal* 46 (1996): 1.

14 *Brown v. Board of Education of Topeka*, 347 U.S. 483 (1954) (outlawing racial segregation in public schools); *Gideon v. Wainwright*, 372 U.S. 335 (1963) (protecting right to counsel for accused persons); *Roe v. Wade*, 410 U.S. 113 (1973) (striking down laws that criminalized abortions).

15 "The Role of Global Law Firms in Constructing or Obstructing a Transnational Regime of Labour Law," in *Rules and Networks: The Legal Culture of Global Business Transactions*, ed. R. Appelbaum, W. Felstiner, and V. Gessner (Oxford: Hart Publishing, 2001), 273.

16 "Private Ordering and Workers' Rights in the Global Economy: Corporate Codes of Conduct as a Regime of Labour Market Regulation," in *Labour Law in an Era of Globalization: Transformative Practices and Possibilities*, ed. J. Conaghan, K. Klare, and M. Fischl (Oxford: Oxford University Press), 471–87, republished in W. Cragg, ed. *Ethics Codes, Corporations and the Challenges of Globalization* (Cheltenham, UK: Edward Elgar Press, 2005); "Corporate Self-regulation: Political Economy, State Regulation and Reflexive Labour Law," in *Regulating Labour in the Wake of Globalisation*, ed. C. Estlund and B. Bercusson (Oxford: Hart Publishing, 2007), 19.

17 "Labour Law and Transnational Law: The Fate of Legal Fields / The Trajectory of Legal Scholarship," in *The London Lectures on Transnational Law and Global Governance: Keynote Lectures from the Inaugural Transnational Law Summer Institute, King's College London*, ed. Prahba Kotiswaran and Peer Zumbansen (Cambridge: Cambridge University Press, 2017).

18 "'Landscape and Memory': Labour Law, Legal Pluralism and Globalization," in *Advancing Theory in Labour Law in a Global Context*, ed. T. Wilthagen (Amsterdam: North Holland Press, 1997), 21.

19   *The New Economy and the Demise of Industrial Citizenship*, 1.

20   See e.g. Michel Coutu, "Industrial Citizenship, Human Rights and the
     Transformation of Labour Law: A Critical Assessment of Harry Arthurs'
     Legalization Thesis," *Canadian Journal of Law & Society* 19 (2004): 73.

21   M.G. Marmot et al., "Employment Grade and Coronary Heart Disease in
     British Civil Servants," *Journal of Epidemiology and Community Health*
     32 (1978): 244; M.G. Marmot et al., "Inequalities in Death – Specific
     Explanations of a General Pattern?" *The Lancet* 8384 (1984): 1003; M.G.
     Marmot et al., "Health Inequalities among British Civil Servants: The
     Whitehall II Study," *The Lancet* 337 (1991): 1387.

22   "Constitutional Courage," *McGill Law Journal* 49 (2003): 3;
     "Constitutionalism – An Idea Whose Time Has Come ... and Gone?"
     Amicus Curiae 75, 3 (2008): 3.

23   Harry Arthurs and Brent Arnold, "Does the Charter Matter?" *Review of
     Constitutional Studies* 11 (2005): 37.

24   "Labour and the 'Real' Constitution," *Cahiers du droit* 48, (2007): 43.

25   '"The Right to Golf": Reflections on the Future of Workers, Unions and
     the Rest of Us under the Charter," *Queen's Law Journal* 13, 2 (1989): 217;
     "Of Skeptics and Idealists: Bernie and Me and the Right to Strike,"
     Canadian Labour & Employment Law Journal 19 (2015–16): 327.

26   "Constitutionalizing the Right of Workers to Organize, Bargain and
     Strike: The Sight of One Shoulder Shrugging," *Canadian Labour &
     Employment Law Journal* 15 (2010): 273.

CHAPTER ELEVEN

1   "Law and Learning in an Age of Globalization," *German Law Journal* 10
    (2014): 629.

Index

Patrons of the Osgoode Society

Blake, Cassels & Graydon, LLP

Chernos, Flaherty, Svorkin, LLP

Gowlings WLG

Hull & Hull

The Law Foundation of Ontario

McCarthy Tétrault LLP

Osler, Hoskin & Harcourt LLP

Paliare Roland Rosenberg Rothstein LLP

Torys LLP

WeirFoulds LLP

Publications of the Osgoode Society for Canadian Legal History

Dominique Clément, *Equality Deferred: Sex Discrimination and British Columbia's Human Rights State, 1953–84*

Paul Craven, *Petty Justice: Low Law and the Sessions System in Charlotte County, New Brunswick, 1785–1867*

Thomas Telfer, *Ruin and Redemption: The Struggle for a Canadian Bankruptcy Law, 1867–1919*

2013 The Hon. R. Roy McMurtry, *Memoirs & Reflections*

Charlotte Gray, *The Massey Murder: A Maid, Her Master and the Trial that Shocked a Nation*

C. Ian Kyer, *Lawyers, Families, and Businesses: The Shaping of a Bay Street Law Firm, Faskens 1863–1963*

G. Blaine Baker and Donald Fyson, eds., *Essays in the History of Canadian Law. Volume 11: Quebec and the Canadas*

2012 R. Blake Brown, *Arming and Disarming: A History of Gun Control in Canada*

Eric Tucker, James Muir, and Bruce Ziff, eds., *Property on Trial: Canadian Cases in Context*

Shelley A.M. Gavigan, *Hunger, Horses, and Government Men: Criminal Law on the Aboriginal Plains, 1870–1905*

Barrington Walker, ed., *The African-Canadian Legal Odyssey: Historical Essays*

2011 Robert J. Sharpe, *The Lazier Murder: Prince Edward County, 1884*

Philip Girard, *Lawyers and Legal Culture in British North America: Beamish Murdoch of Halifax*

John McLaren, *Dewigged, Bothered and Bewildered: British Colonial Judges on Trial*

Lesley Erickson, *Westward Bound: Sex, Violence, the Law, and the Making of a Settler Society*

2010 Judy Fudge and Eric Tucker, eds., *Work on Trial: Canadian Labour Law Struggles*

Christopher Moore, *The British Columbia Court of Appeal: The First Hundred Years*

Frederick Vaughan, *Viscount Haldane: The Wicked Step-father of the Canadian Constitution*

Barrington Walker, *Race on Trial: Black Defendants in Ontario's Criminal Courts, 1850–1950*

2009 William Kaplan, *Canadian Maverick: The Life and Times of Ivan C. Rand*

R. Blake Brown, *A Trying Question: The Jury in Nineteenth-Century Canada*

Barry Wright and Susan Binnie, eds., *Canadian State Trials. Volume 3: Political Trials and Security Measures, 1840–1914*

Robert J. Sharpe, *The Last Day, the Last Hour: The Currie Libel Trial*

2008 Constance Backhouse, *Carnal Crimes: Sexual Assault Law in Canada, 1900–1975*

Jim Phillips, R. Roy McMurtry, and John Saywell, eds., *Essays in the History of Canadian Law. Volume 10: A Tribute to Peter N. Oliver*

Gregory Taylor, *The Law of the Land: Canada's Receptions of the Torrens System*

Hamar Foster, Benjamin Berger, and A.R. Buck, eds., *The Grand Experiment: Law and Legal Culture in British Settler Societies*

2007 Robert Sharpe and Patricia McMahon, *The Persons Case: The Origins and Legacy of the Fight for Legal Personhood*

Lori Chambers, *Misconceptions: Unmarried Motherhood and the Ontario Children of Unmarried Parents Act, 1921–1969*

Jonathan Swainger, ed., *The Alberta Supreme Court at 100: History and Authority*

Martin Friedland, *My Life in Crime and Other Academic Adventures*

2006 Donald Fyson, *Magistrates, Police and People: Everyday Criminal Justice in Quebec and Lower Canada, 1764–1837*

Dale Brawn, *The Court of Queen's Bench of Manitoba 1870–1950: A Biographical History*

R.C.B. Risk, *A History of Canadian Legal Thought: Collected Essays,* edited and introduced by G. Blaine Baker and Jim Phillips

2005 Philip Girard, *Bora Laskin: Bringing Law to Life*

Christopher English, ed., *Essays in the History of Canadian Law. Volume 9: Two Islands, Newfoundland and Prince Edward Island*

Fred Kaufman, *Searching for Justice: An Autobiography*

2004 John D. Honsberger, *Osgoode Hall: An Illustrated History*

Frederick Vaughan, *Aggressive in Pursuit: The Life of Justice Emmett Hall*

Constance Backhouse and Nancy Backhouse, *The Heiress versus the Establishment: Mrs. Campbell's Campaign for Legal Justice*

Philip Girard, Jim Phillips, and Barry Cahill, eds., *The Supreme Court of Nova Scotia, 1754–2004: From Imperial Bastion to Provincial Oracle*

2003 Robert Sharpe and Kent Roach, *Brian Dickson: A Judge's Journey*
George Finlayson, *John J. Robinette: Peerless Mentor*
Peter Oliver, *The Conventional Man: The Diaries of Ontario Chief Justice Robert A. Harrison, 1856–1878*
Jerry Bannister, *The Rule of the Admirals: Law, Custom and Naval Government in Newfoundland, 1699–1832*

2002 John T. Saywell, *The Law Makers: Judicial Power and the Shaping of Canadian Federalism*
David Murray, *Colonial Justice: Justice, Morality and Crime in the Niagara District, 1791–1849*
F. Murray Greenwood and Barry Wright, eds., *Canadian State Trials. Volume 2: Rebellion and Invasion in the Canadas, 1837–38*
Patrick Brode, *Courted and Abandoned: Seduction in Canadian Law*

2001 Ellen Anderson, *Judging Bertha Wilson: Law as Large as Life*
Judy Fudge and Eric Tucker, *Labour before the Law: Collective Action in Canada, 1900–1948*
Laurel Sefton MacDowell, *Renegade Lawyer: The Life of J.L. Cohen*

2000 Barry Cahill, *"The Thousandth Man": A Biography of James McGregor Stewart*
A.B. McKillop, *The Spinster and the Prophet: Florence Deeks, H.G. Wells, and the Mystery of the Purloined Past*
Beverley Boissery and F. Murray Greenwood, *Uncertain Justice: Canadian Women and Capital Punishment*
Bruce Ziff, *Unforeseen Legacies: Reuben Wells Leonard and the Leonard Foundation Trust*

1999 Constance Backhouse, *Colour-Coded: A Legal History of Racism in Canada, 1900–1950*
G. Blaine Baker and Jim Phillips, eds., *Essays in the History of Canadian Law. Volume 8: In Honour of R.C.B. Risk*
Richard W. Pound, *Chief Justice W.R. Jackett: By the Law of the Land*
David Vanek, *Fulfilment: Memoirs of a Criminal Court Judge*

1998 Sidney Harring, *White Man's Law: Native People in Nineteenth-Century Canadian Jurisprudence*
Peter Oliver, *"Terror to Evil-Doers": Prisons and Punishments in Nineteenth-Century Ontario*

1997 James W. St. G. Walker, *"Race," Rights and the Law in the Supreme Court of Canada: Historical Case Studies*

Lori Chambers, *Married Women and Property Law in Victorian Ontario*

Patrick Brode, *Casual Slaughters and Accidental Judgments: Canadian War Crimes and Prosecutions, 1944–1948*

Ian Bushnell, *The Federal Court of Canada: A History, 1875–1992*

1996 Carol Wilton, ed., *Essays in the History of Canadian Law. Volume 7: Inside the Law -- Canadian Law Firms in Historical Perspective*

William Kaplan, *Bad Judgment: The Case of Mr. Justice Leo A. Landreville*

Murray Greenwood and Barry Wright, eds., *Canadian State Trials. Volume 1: Law, Politics and Security Measures, 1608–1837*

1995 David Williams, *Just Lawyers: Seven Portraits*

Hamar Foster and John McLaren, eds., *Essays in the History of Canadian Law. Volume 6: British Columbia and the Yukon*

W.H. Morrow, ed., *Northern Justice: The Memoirs of Mr. Justice William G. Morrow*

Beverley Boissery, *A Deep Sense of Wrong: The Treason, Trials and Transportation to New South Wales of Lower Canadian Rebels after the 1838 Rebellion*

1994 Patrick Boyer, *A Passion for Justice: The Legacy of James Chalmers McRuer*

Charles Pullen, *The Life and Times of Arthur Maloney: The Last of the Tribunes*

Jim Phillips, Tina Loo, and Susan Lewthwaite, eds., *Essays in the History of Canadian Law. Volume 5: Crime and Criminal Justice*

Brian Young, *The Politics of Codification: The Lower Canadian Civil Code of 1866*

1993 Greg Marquis, *Policing Canada's Century: A History of the Canadian Association of Chiefs of Police*

Murray Greenwood, *Legacies of Fear: Law and Politics in Quebec in the Era of the French Revolution*

1992 Brendan O'Brien, *Speedy Justice: The Tragic Last Voyage of His Majesty's Vessel* Speedy

Robert Fraser, ed., *Provincial Justice: Upper Canadian Legal Portraits from the* Dictionary of Canadian Biography

1991 Constance Backhouse, *Petticoats and Prejudice: Women and Law in Nineteenth-Century Canada*

1990 Philip Girard and Jim Phillips, eds., *Essays in the History of Canadian Law. Volume 3: Nova Scotia*

Carol Wilton, ed., *Essays in the History of Canadian Law. Volume 4: Beyond the Law – Lawyers and Business in Canada 1830–1930*

1989 Desmond Brown, *The Genesis of the Canadian Criminal Code of 1892*

Patrick Brode, *The Odyssey of John Anderson*

1988 Robert Sharpe, *The Last Day, the Last Hour: The Currie Libel Trial*

John D. Arnup, *Middleton: The Beloved Judge*

1987 C. Ian Kyer and Jerome Bickenbach, *The Fiercest Debate: Cecil A. Wright, the Benchers and Legal Education in Ontario, 1923–1957*

1986 Paul Romney, *Mr. Attorney: The Attorney General for Ontario in Court, Cabinet and Legislature, 1791–1899*

Martin Friedland, *The Case of Valentine Shortis: A True Story of Crime and Politics in Canada*

1985 James Snell and Frederick Vaughan, *The Supreme Court of Canada: History of the Institution*

1984 Patrick Brode, *Sir John Beverley Robinson: Bone and Sinew of the Compact*

David Williams, *Duff: A Life in the Law*

1983 David H. Flaherty, ed., *Essays in the History of Canadian Law. Volume 2*

1982 Marion MacRae and Anthony Adamson, *Cornerstones of Order: Courthouses and Town Halls of Ontario, 1784–1914*

1981 David H. Flaherty, ed., *Essays in the History of Canadian Law. Volume 1*